LIVE BEAUTIFUL

LIVE BEAUTIFUL

ATHENA CALDERONE

FOREWORD BY AMY ASTLEY
PHOTOGRAPHY BY NICOLE FRANZEN

—

ABRAMS, NEW YORK

FOREWORD

BY AMY ASTLEY

Athena Calderone is my friend who really can do it all. She is an actual domestic goddess—emphasis on both words.

Athena's first book, *Cook Beautiful,* proved her fierce kitchen bona fides. Thanks to Athena's passion for photography, styling, and setting a glorious table, her food looks just as good as it tastes. This second book, *Live Beautiful,* reveals a flip (yet complementary) side to Athena the chef: Athena the gifted and intuitive interior designer, who has created several enviably photogenic homes for her family.

But don't hate her because she lives beautiful! Athena's secret weapon is her generosity—she is a sharer. She wants her readers, followers, and friends to make their personal world as delicious, attractive, and joyful as her own. Just look at her site or any of her Instagram posts (the entire enterprise aptly named EyeSwoon) and you will discover a natural writer and storyteller, one who openly confesses her own insecurities and challenges (in kitchen, home, and career), while unreservedly dispensing recipes, decorating tips, style hacks, and life advice. Sure, Athena's taste is elevated and aspirational, but her tone is unpretentious and inclusive—she wants you to have what she is having! Ease, simplicity, and approachability are her mantra. And she often notes that beautiful does not necessarily mean complicated. Or expensive.

In this book, Athena has persuaded nineteen international "creatives" who have inspired her to open their doors.

Documenting the homes of fellow influencers like Jenna Lyons, Nate Berkus and Jeremiah Brent, and Stephen Alesch and Robin Standefer (the husband-and-wife duo behind Roman and Williams) with that signature clean-yet-dreamy EyeSwoon photography by Nicole Franzen, Athena unpacks the personal style and clever solutions behind each space. The accompanying text, in her clear and instructional, yet warmly affirmational voice, offers up practical DIY suggestions for anyone eager to reimagine their own environment.

When *Architectural Digest* published Athena's Cobble Hill townhouse in late 2018, the story instantly became a digital sensation—her light, bright, and luxuriously windowed kitchen alone surely launched a million Pinterest boards. It has been fascinating and fun to see how both that space and Athena's much-admired Amagansett beach house keep evolving as they function as laboratories for her stylistic experiments and growth. The same can be said for the residences Athena has selected to record in this book. Some are familiar, some completely fresh to the eye, but all pass the Athena taste test: they share a spare, lean-yet-luscious aesthetic and feel simultaneously current and classic. Athena has the seemingly effortless ability to intuit—and exemplify—just how people want to decorate and eat today. She makes it so easy for the rest of us to live beautiful.

INTRO—
DUCTION

I have always been intrigued by the behind-the-scenes: the hidden process of how things magically come together and the spark of inspiration that incites a journey. When it comes to the design of our homes—and the carefully curated objects that comprise them—what intrigues me most is how the decisions that lead to an end result are rarely obvious. The aesthetics we create are an accumulation of seemingly small decor influences—a sofa you first spied in a shelter magazine that sent you on a hunt, ancient Greek columns that solved a hallway dilemma, or a mural that guides the painterly palette of your home. From a wellspring of inspiration, a dialogue begins, and the language of a room takes form, gently carrying you to the next decision. I want to amplify these quieter creative moments, because they are far louder than they seem. These are the choices that reflect our individuality and shape the alchemy in our homes.

You know how you can initially be moved by a piece of art, and yet gain a far stronger attachment once you learn about the artist's approach? This is precisely how I feel about design. Oftentimes, this visual chemistry is difficult to articulate. It is the composition and silent space in between things, a wordless expression, a hybrid of contrasts that can cause both tension and curiosity. It is a personal journey steeped in spontaneity and trusting our eye.

In my work, I continually ask other creatives to pull back the curtain on their design practices. I want to better understand the fluidity of their process and the principles at play: How do you achieve the right balance of scale, texture, patina, and layering? Is it the mix of materials, periods, or styles? Is it the blend of high and low? Is it intuitive or more studied? Is it worth staying true to the architecture of the house, or is

it better to diverge to reflect your own tastes? Understanding each fork in the road is fascinating and enlightening to me. The path is full of twists and turns.

Through the prism of the creatives in this book, I found beauty—the intrinsic essence of which is both intangible and highly personal. Not only did it teach me something about their unique lens on the aesthetic world around us, but, more important, it also helped me understand my own eye. Each designer here—through an accumulation of gestures, anecdotes, and histories—brings a version of living beautiful to life. In summoning all of these sumptuous, enigmatic homes together, I'm trying to understand as much about them as I am about conscious or unconscious design practices at play, not in an effort to mimic, but rather to help inform my own process. To Live Beautiful simply means to tinker with, explore, and ultimately find your own design gold at home. While beauty is different for each of the nineteen creatives I've interviewed, the journey for achieving it is remarkably similar— design unfolds piece by piece in an intuitive, emotional, and heartfelt process.

As much as this book is about intimate creative portraits, it is also a practical deep dive, offering actionable ideas that will help you design your home. The inspiring photography here is accompanied by extractable tips on "why the design works," the resources each homeowner drew from, and teacherly insight to help you understand the principles at play. Whether you are embarking on a gut renovation like Pamela Shamshiri or renting an apartment you can't alter like Signe Bindslev Henriksen, *Live Beautiful* will hopefully inspire and help you make choices in your own home, no matter your budget.

MY OWN DESIGN EVOLUTION

Over the past twenty years, I have owned and renovated eight homes. Yes, I am the rare bird who moves every two to three years and thoroughly enjoys every bit of it! Some may find the thought of ping-ponging around Brooklyn—as we have—to be unsettling. But to our family of three, it just feels natural and exciting. Every home has allowed me to strengthen my architecture and design muscles. I love to reinvent a space. I get silly excited by the all-encompassing research and find the scavenging and collecting of objects downright thrilling. I fixate on the problem-solving until I find resolution, and I crave the knowledge these renovations offer me. Most of all, I love the journey. It's exhilarating—if you allow yourself to be led.

This acute appreciation for design likely began when I was a child growing up in our modest ranch-style home on Long Island, New York. My mom would rearrange the furniture on a weekly basis. Never complacent, she continually made small tweaks to improve and experiment with the aesthetics of our house. I'd often walk into a room only to find the floor-plan flip-flopped. It was exciting to be a bystander to these transformations and experience the ways in which a layout, a color, or a piece of furniture could completely alter a space.

As an adult, my foray into design and real estate began in Dumbo, Brooklyn, in 1998; over the years, each home became a reflection of my changing tastes and our needs as a family of three. By 2006, I embarked on my third renovation in Dumbo, which was also my most ambitious yet—and it led me to believe that perhaps I needed to explore interiors further. When our son was three, I went back to school at Parsons to study interior design. Within a year, I cofounded my own interior design business, Rawlins Calderone Design. While I learned invaluable lessons working for clients, it was within my own homes that I learned to trust my instincts. I never wanted to repeat myself, so in each home, I explored a new style. My homes throughout the years became my design laboratory: Amagansett—rustic modernity (page 139)— and Cobble Hill—sophisticated form (page 17). Actualizing a vision, seeing it go from concept to fruition, was something I found incredibly rewarding.

KNOWLEDGE IS POWER

Just as in cooking, a home is made up of simple, raw ingredients—architecture, finishes, and furnishings. Once united, they become greater than the sum of their parts. Each element elevates what sits beside it, turning it into something new. These often-invisible steps can be unmasked and shared, kindling exploration in others. A chain reaction that leads to a decision is unique to each of us. At the home of Gabriel Hendifar and Jeremy Anderson, a chance find of a pastoral Danish mural became the design catalyst for their loft, informing not only their color palette but even the physical contours of the space. In Jenna Lyons's apartment (opposite), Italian firm Dimore Studio encouraged not just her unapologetic color mixing, but also the unexpected use of brass in her kitchen. These lightning-rod moments of inspiration have the power to become nothing short of contagious.

My website, EyeSwoon, was born in 2011 when I was awash in design inspiration after the overhaul of our midcentury-modern beach house on the East End of Long Island. It was a lesson in exploration and unrelenting inquisitiveness, yielding beautiful results. As I elaborate in the chapter on page 139, I mitigated the austerity of the modern architecture by utilizing rope in novel ways. My old design partner used to call me a "super sleuth," because after seeing something I swooned over, I would fixate on it until I found a way to make it a reality.

DESIGN FINGERPRINTS

We live in such a visually saturated time, our eyes feeding our creativity and recording everything that intrigues us. I believe images get stashed away in little drawers in our mind. We all borrow from one another, don't we? We take bits and bobs of other people's genius and filter them through our own lens and into our homes. In seemingly spontaneous bursts of inspiration, we never know when one of these drawers will fly open to reveal a brilliant idea. When Giancarlo Valle and Jane Keltner de Valle visited a local Connecticut shop, they were awestruck by a marble Gae Aulenti table that inadvertently triggered a memory of an iconic David Hicks–designed room. It ultimately shaped the direction of their family room. This cascade of inspiration is design magic to me.

In this book, I ask each homeowner and designer about the inspiration, travel, art, objects, photographs, and stories that have illuminated their design pathway. The pieces they've collected over time tell us about more than their taste in furnishings—they reveal the contours of life's path, like a visual diary. In the home of Nate Berkus and Jeremiah Brent (opposite), a collection of patina-rich pots hailing from Peru to Vietnam tell the tale of their travels, transporting them to a place and a time at every glance. My own homes tell a story of precious memories from my evolution as woman, wife, mother, and designer. They reflect my past and will hold my future. Most every piece in my homes conjures a time or place, triggering the journey of its origin, while its placement and juxtaposition reveals that which excites my eye.

The items we choose to surround ourselves with are profoundly intimate. We collect what resonates with us without always knowing where it may eventually land, but each object holds such power in the greater universe of our inimitable home. The way we arrange the pieces we bring into our home—and their significance—is unique to us. Even if two people acquire the same object, that treasure is only a starting place. It will live on in our homes in deeply personal ways. Being the seeker that I am, I want to understand design in its most personal form—how others have followed their intuition, and how their spaces have unfolded. On a higher level, I want to illustrate the ways in which great design can improve the quality of our lives. Selfishly, I am also simply curious about other people's design journeys—because understanding another's process helps me define and refine what Live Beautiful means to me. I hope you are as intrigued as I am.

ATHENA AND VICTOR

FACT SHEET

Athena Calderone:
Designer. Visual and Culinary
Storyteller

Victor Calderone:
Music Producer and DJ

Children:
Jivan

Cobble Hill
Brooklyn, New York

Late 1800s, Greek Revival

Specs:
4,000 square feet
3 bedrooms
3 bathrooms
1 office
1 recording studio
1 family room

RESOURCES

Beloved Antique Dealer
MORENTZ *(The Netherlands)*
PHEROMONES *(Saint-Ouen, France)*
GALERIE FRADIN-LABROSSE *(Paris)*

Contemporary Designer or Shop
DEMIURGE *(New York)*
RW GUILD *(New York)*
APPARATUS *(New York)*
GIANCARLO VALLE *(New York)*

Favorite Linens/Bedding
COYUCHI ORGANIC BEDDING

Go-To for Tabletop
JONO PANDOLFI
IL BUCO VITA GLASSES
CUTIPOL FLATWARE

Paint Brand/Color
FARROW & BALL: RAILINGS
PORTOLA PAINTS: IN THE NAVY

Online Destination for Decor
BLACK CREEK MERCANTILE
   & TRADING CO.
PERSPECTIVE STUDIO
ARNO DECLERCQ *(Belgium)*

Favorite Gallery, Flea Market,
or Auction House
PASADENA ANTIQUE CENTER
   (Pasadena)
1STDIBS *(online)*
GALERIE HALF *(Los Angeles)*

"I WAS ITCHING TO GET MY HANDS ON SOMETHING THAT SCARED ME A BIT—MASSIVE, DAUNTING, AND TANTALIZING."

This townhouse is my design epic. It's been an intention and a distant dream for years. Miraculously, it manifested itself four years ago, and its realization—from renovation, to decoration, to the education it fomented—gripped my life for three of them. The journey to here—to home—is the culmination of all my time spent looking, seeking, and yearning for that which my eye craves. It is my masterpiece, second only to being my family's sanctuary.

The townhouse, a late 1800s Greek Revival, needed a lot of love. It had been stripped of much of its original detail when it was fractured and converted into four apartments. But its twenty-five-foot-wide girth (average brownstones clock in at eighteen to twenty feet) on a tree-lined, historic street—and southern exposure and proximity to Manhattan—made it an absolute catch. I had always fantasized about designing a townhouse—fusing ornate traditional architecture with my idea of modern living (complemented by my nonconform-ist stamp on it, of course). I imagined inserting the old-world details of the many Copenhagen and Parisian apartments I had swooned over, grand double doors and all, and marrying them to a Brooklyn sensibility that juxtaposed the grandeur and grit of the city's yesteryear. I was also itching to get my hands on something that scared me a bit, something new. I knew that a clash of cultures in the decor was essential for this home—a mix of mostly Italian and French antiques rang-ing from the forties through the seventies. But I also desired the age and patina of the eighteenth century sprinkled in here and there to drive home a sense of history. This became my template.

I approached this renovation leading with what excites me most—decor. Where I began was never where I ended up. I mean, how fun is seeking to find that "thing" we don't even know we are looking for? We think we know, but we don't, cerebrally anyway; only our eye knows when we see it. The accumulation of each and every piece in my home was a granular alchemic experiment of trusting my eye. Like an animal on the hunt—voracious, calculating, patient, and precise—I searched. Hours became days, which became weeks, and then years, scouring Chairish, 1stdibs, auction sites, eBay, Instagram, estate sales from the Hamptons to Miami. I obsessively e-mailed dealers, and aesthetic wander-lust found me on planes throughout Europe to accumulate pieces I did not know I needed so desperately in my life until I saw them.

While I was guided by my passion for the interior picture, that's not to say I wasn't committed to addressing our prac-tical needs, either. We collaborated with Elizabeth Roberts Architecture and began to dissect our specific desires as a family. My first step, and one I encourage every homeowner to take, was to create a comprehensive list—floor by floor, room by room—of our collective and individual needs. Every minute detail was added, and it helped us understand how to divvy up the space and determine the ideal location and purpose for every room.

Victor and I agreed that opening up the parlor floor to bring in as much light as possible was essential. Not only do we thrive on sunshine, but the natural light is imperative for my work photographing vignettes and shooting video. This meant

"THE SPACE FEELS COHESIVE, WITH LOTS TO LOOK AT—THINGS SORT OF DISAPPEAR OR COME INTO FOCUS, DEPENDING ON WHERE I WANTED YOUR EYE TO LAND."

taking down the weight-bearing wall that divided the stairway from the rest of the space. With southern exposure and an odd L-shaped configuration at the back of the house, I knew I wanted the kitchen to dominate the rear of the home.

To achieve a bright and grand kitchen, we installed a wall of floor-to-ceiling metal casement windows that would dramatically carry light through the entire space. This open floor plan put the living room, dining room, and kitchen all in one long expanse. That's a lot of functionality stacked within one floor. Without walls to serve as boundaries, I needed to find a way to make each area feel intimate and distinct, yet cohesive. Here is where architecture, design, and decor unite.

Patience being a decorative virtue, I exercised restraint, never making hasty decisions unless something spoke to me with clarity. That isn't to say I wasn't obsessive. In every home there is a struggle one must grapple with; for me, it was finding a lighting solution for three distinct living areas on the parlor floor—something that would be harmonious from each area to the next. Like Goldilocks and the three bears, I tried and tested options—three of the same pendant lights, recessed lighting (in hindsight, yuck!), even forgoing one entirely in the front parlor (but what is a Brooklyn townhouse without a jaw-dropping chandelier to admire from the street?). It all felt like a concession, and I wasn't willing to concede. In an attempt to fill a void, I put a tall, fluted vessel filled with seasonal sculptural branches on the kitchen island. This work-around offered verticality, drama, and nature, and it liberated me to focus on finding just the right symbiosis between the living and dining areas.

The search continued. I had fallen down a plaster rabbit hole, exhaustively educating myself on Alberto Giacometti's breath-taking body of work. A plaster chandelier would be a beautiful and monochromatic foil to the original ornately scrolled medallion in the living room—and it wouldn't compete with the dining room. I couldn't afford a Giacometti, but obsessive searching led me to Demiurge. I chose a cylindrical design and floral stem that most closely recalled my original inspiration. Observations lead to research, and decisions carry us to the next.

On my master floor, architecture informed the space. Grand double doors led to the master bathroom, boasting an old-world-style bathtub, plaster walls, and marble fireplace, but the hallway in between served no purpose. This demanded a statement. I explored wallpaper, a mural, decorative hooks—nothing felt right. Obsessed with collecting plinths and pillars for the home, I was attracted to ancient Greek marble columns, but it wasn't until I saw a wood-paneled room at the University of Padua designed by Gio Ponti that I found what I was after. I wrapped fluted plaster up the walls and over the ceiling, drawing the eye to the room's focal point: the bathtub.

For our family room, I craved a formal library, but with the comfort to slouch into a plush sofa and watch movies or read as a family. The initial vision was in line with the neutral tonality of the home, but something wasn't working. The room felt incomplete, so we enveloped the walls and ceiling in deeply saturated navy plaster, which offered a suede-like quality. The dark hue demanded furniture that was equally weighted in form and color; we added a bespoke sofa

MOMENT *to* MOMENT

Vignettes bring a story to the home, forming a narrative in their grouping. Here, on the left, a tall vintage parchment planter is placed on its own, offering vertical interest. Object placement on the right provides differentiation not only in height, but also in color, texture, age, form, and tonality. Recognize what can stand alone and what needs friends. The planter is a tall, sculptural object that lives happily alone. But the objects on the right, if they were unmoored from one another, would lose their value, looking oddly diminutive in contrast. Consider scale and negative space.

designed by Giancarlo Valle and a jewel-toned fringed chair and velvet ottoman inspired by Milanese design. Once transformed, the room became the cozy nook it wanted to be.

In distilling this house, I offer a few tried-and-true guiding principles I follow when conceptualizing a space. My design philosophy continuously plays with contrast and cohesion. I find that for design to be successful, there needs to be a synthesis of both elements reacting off of one another. I love to pair objects that oppose each other in some capacity— I believe there is a certain level of voltage that happens when you juxtapose an item that is feminine, soft, tactile, and curvaceous against a piece that is inherently more masculine, hard-lined, and bold in its material or form.

Patina—the worn quality that reveals an object's untold history—is another way to bring friction to an interior. I constantly strive to find the right balance of patina and polish. A pair of timeworn, rugged stone vessels lives on my credenza. By placing them next to a modernist, graphic, and linear piece of art, I am amplifying that contradiction. In the corner of the parlor floor, I paired a tall, square-shaped Swedish plinth stripped of its paint to reveal the wood underneath with a low marble column. Together their composition is odd, interesting, and unexpected. The alchemy is design magic. Juxtaposing scale can have a marvelous effect, causing your eye to leapfrog about the room, engaging your interest and breaking monotony.

Another tenet is the hunt. I am asked a countless number of times where I found something—99 percent of the time,

the response is: "It's vintage." That doesn't mean it's expensive or precious, but rather, it's finding something that touches you in some way. Let your eye lead you and find the joy in hunting for pieces that excite you. Educate your eye and build your internal visual library. Study what you love about a particular room. When you discover something similar, acquire it and alter it if need be. Peruse a corner junk shop or eBay for hidden treasures, because there is no one place to find beauty.

Allow color and texture to speak for you, designating places of calm, and highlighting ecstatic moments. My bedroom envelops you in serenity with its neutral palette. In contrast, I strategically introduced a duo of vibrant colors—the warm mustard hue from the chair and the wine-red bench—to focus your attention. In my kitchen, I use minimalism to draw your eyes to the elements I deem most important. With no upper cabinets, the textural plaster finish offers refined negative space, allowing functional and decorative items to pop, including my beloved sconces.

I give you these examples not so you can emulate my style, but to help you cultivate your inner vision. This townhouse was my education in design. Studying some of the greats that were completely unattainable for me, like Royère, Jean-Michel Frank, Brancusi, and Giacometti, helped me understand what I was drawn to, gave me confidence, and allowed me to define what I love about design, what excites me most, and how I want to live in my spaces.

Broken PLANES

You never want your furniture and objects to be on the same plane. My living room, which isn't stuffed with things, feels rich and layered. I achieved this by uniting furniture and objects that are all at different heights. The low sofa, two-tiered triangular coffee table, closely stacked pillars, sculptural standing lamp, and Prouvé stool draw your eyes around the room, bouncing from point to point, lending it a playful allure. Think about varying scale when designing a room.

BEAT TO *Your Own* DRUM

Hire a professional, and don't be afraid to alter a finish. The detailing of an iconic Jacques Adnet sideboard made my heart sing, but its original chestnut color did not. I also loved the silhouette of Niels Møller's classic chairs, but not their rosewood finish. Undeterred, I had my Adnet piece stripped and bleached to suit my color scheme (causing a gasp among my design-savvy friends) and my Møller chairs dyed black.

AIR UP *There*

If you choose to eliminate upper cabinets as I did, maintain that minimal sensibility. Open kitchen shelving can easily look cluttered, so leave it airy up top. Use pale textured plaster or paint as a canvas on which decorative items can pop and functional items, like the hood, disappear. Dark lower cabinets will also recede, focusing your gaze on the pieces you've chosen to display.

OBJECT OF *My* AFFECTION

Inject more decorative pieces into a functional space. Mirrors, lamps, and art can and should live within your kitchen. Don't rob your functional spaces of beautiful objects. Everyone always ends up gathering here. Why not have that decorative element in your most used and heartfelt space?

Worth THE WAIT

Allow your eyes time to see things differently and embrace an unexpected solution. I had a clear vision for the design in the kitchen, but I continued to vacillate on the pendant over the island. It was in the waiting that I realized I didn't want a pendant at all. I filled a vintage vessel with seasonal branches, which brought the outdoors in and offered unexpected verticality to what was once a confusing void.

Set IN STONE

Some design decisions need to be addressed during the renovation. I pined after the heavily veined marble
I spied in Joseph Dirand's Parisian kitchen that forms a free-floating shelf. In emulating this, I learned that
this device has to be supported with braced walls. Think about stone application early in your process,
especially if you are after bracket-free shelving.

ROOM *with* A VIEW

No one covets a floor-to-ceiling window more than a New Yorker. While it might seem counterintuitive to have obscured it, I installed a floating soapstone "desk" in front of the expansive window that punctuates the end of my kitchen. In doing so, I am actually highlighting the window—and its lush Brooklyn-jungle backyard view—and creating a truly dreamy work space.

Super SLEUTH

Never underestimate the power of Google. Of course, it's easy to find something you love at a highly curated purveyor, like the antique stone floor that I was eyeing from a famed showroom. Undeterred, a few Google searches later, I found a similar style of marble and travertine from a stone yard in New Jersey for a third of the price. Seek and ye shall find.

"I ALWAYS ASK MYSELF, WHAT DO I WANT TO CONJURE IN THIS SPACE? I CAN'T CONTROL PEOPLE'S EMOTIONS, BUT I CAN CONTROL THE MOOD OF MY HOME."

HALLWAYS ARE ROOMS, *Too*

Transitional spaces—stairways, hallways, landings—are often wasted design opportunities. In this hallway, which leads to our bedroom, I cut a console in half to fit the hall's shallow depth and used it as an anchor, while a plinth with a vessel tucked into the landing corner adds a statuesque quality. Search for furniture with a thin profile and consider retrofitting to accommodate your space. Hallways are also ideal places to play with verticality.

"NEUTRAL, ON NEUTRAL, ON TEXTURE, ON TEXTURE, CAN IN FACT BE RICH AND LAYERED."

GENDER *Dynamics*

Yin and yang. Masculine and feminine. There is friction to be found in playing with extremes. Our bathroom, boasting old European charm, took on a decidedly feminine identity with its pink-veined marble, 1930s Murano chandelier resembling a flower's stamen, and romantic freestanding bathtub. I intentionally contrasted the daintiness by injecting harsh black elements—window frames, vanity mirrors (which I painted myself), and a range of vessels. I also introduced strong sculptural forms, like a nude male torso and strident sconces.

TEENAGE *Dream*

Designing a room for your child who is transitioning to a mini adult can come with lots of opinions. Negotiate a truce in which you both come out on top. He wanted all black; we settled on gray. He wanted an extra bed without a juvenile bunk; we settled on a platform with a hidden trundle. He wanted super modern and a display for his sneakers; we settled on unfinished plywood and built-ins to unify the bed, closet, and desk. I also padded the walls for comfy video game playing, and, in support of his photography hobby, I blew up his own work to anchor the space as his own.

A *Good* SHELFIE

Bookshelves should be like curiosity cabinets—filled with books and objects meaningful to you. Create vignettes by pairing various heights and shapes. Stack books in uneven parallel and perpendicular lines, clustered by subject and spine color. Orient each shelf differently from the one adjacent to it, and add the offbeat (like something found in nature that does not "belong") to move your eye about the bookcase. If you get overwhelmed, step back and take a photo to assess it as an entire tableau.

NATE AND JEREMIAH

FACT SHEET

Nate Berkus:
Designer and Author

Jeremiah Brent:
Designer and TV Personality

Children:
Poppy Brent-Berkus
Oskar Brent-Berkus
Tucker (dog)

Hancock Park
Los Angeles, CA

Spanish Colonial, built in 1928

Specs:
8,500 square feet
5 bedrooms
4 full bathrooms
2 half bathrooms

RESOURCES

Beloved Antique Dealer
PASADENA ANTIQUES
  & DESIGN *(Pasadena)*
BLEND INTERIORS *(Los Angeles)*
HOLLYWOOD AT HOME
  (Los Angeles)
GALERIE HALF *(Los Angeles)*

Contemporary Designer or Shop
APPARATUS *(New York)*
ATELIER MVM *(Los Angeles)*

Favorite Linens/Bedding
MATTEO BEDDING
PRATESI BEDDING

Go-To for Tabletop
REBEKAH MILES HAND-
  PAINTED CERAMIC PLATES
HAND-BLOWN ITALIAN
  GLASSWARE BY GIBERTO
  ARRIVABENE
FLATWARE BY GEORG JENSEN

Paint Brand/Color
BENJAMIN MOORE: ALABASTER
  AND SMOKEY TAUPE
PORTOLA PAINTS: ROMAN CLAY

Online Destination for Decor
1STDIBS
CHAIRISH
ETSY
THE REALREAL

Favorite Gallery, Flea Market,
or Auction House
ANDRÉ VIANA *(New York)*
MARCHÉ PAUL BERT SERPETTE
  (Paris)
LESLIE HINDMAN AUCTIONEERS
  (Chicago) (NATE'S FIRST JOB)
MANTIQUES MODERN *(New York)*
  (FOR THE BEST SMALL
  ACCESSORIES)

"SEEING SOMETHING NEW AND INNOVATIVE IN A SPACE THAT FEELS OLD, SEEING PEOPLE LIVE A LIFE THAT'S MODERN BY DEFINITION IN A SPACE THAT ISN'T, IS RIVETING TO US BOTH."

"The house is still moving around. We created spaces based on moments that we imagined and then we moved in here and realized we're not having the moments in that space," says Jeremiah Brent. Sometimes, we need to live in a home for a bit to really understand the space's true potential and what changes can be made to live our best life between its walls. This is a beautiful truth that highly revered interior designers recognize—like two of my dearest friends, Nate Berkus and Jeremiah Brent. In addition to having the most impeccably curated, well-traveled, and soulfully executed taste level, they have been a sounding board throughout my own design evolution.

Entering the home, the layers unspool before me—each room, each vignette is a tour de force of texture, emotion, history, and most important, the personal. You feel it in every vessel, string of beads, and tactile woven textile, a testament to Jeremiah's love of ritual and Nate's lifelong love of travel. During a trip the two took to Venice in 2017, Jeremiah fell in love with a friend's library strewn with books, objects, worn sofas, and even a veneer of dust. They came home with an epiphany about their dining room. With its grand oak millwork, the formality of the space felt incongruent to the way they live. "We never had one dinner in there," remembers Jeremiah. They realized that the intimacy of the built-ins, however,

and the enveloping wood would make for a rich and cozy library, while a transitional room nearby could act as a lively dining room for entertaining guests. The overhaul of these two rooms took on a fever pitch, and consequently the rooms burst into life. Their dining table and incredible set of twelve Jacques Adnet chairs were reinvigorated under the elaborate coffered ceiling of the new dining room. The library, where they now read to Poppy before bed, is the most layered room in the house. It boasts Nate's voluminous, color-coded, and categorized book collection and Jeremiah's crystals and devotional beads. It has become the melding repository of their most personal interests and objects.

While their library celebrates the personal, their living room could be a case study in harmonizing contrasts. This is what they do really, really well. Four distinct areas coalesce not through style, but color. At the heart of the room, a 1970s Afra and Tobia Scarpa sofa faces 1940s club chairs. To the left of the fireplace, a marble-top table is flanked by English high-back nineteenth-century chairs. A Louis XVI–style daybed is centered under the expansive windows, while an English bench is offset by a midcentury Italian sconce. It is a dazzling display of aesthetic eras and textures, yet they live in harmony, like the range of notes in a symphony. Nate and Jeremiah harness these disparate elements by employing a controlled color

About-FACE

Don't be afraid to change your mind: decorate as you live. If a room isn't living up to its purpose or potential, like Nate and Jeremiah's dining room, consider changing it. Transforming a room's function to better suit your needs can change how you interact with your home—and present an exciting new design opportunity.

palette; nearly everything is cream, black, white, or some gradation therein. Color is a masterful peacemaker. The array of aesthetic influences used in one room parallels their belief that a room should serve more than one function.

Throughout the home, patina is everywhere. "We always reach for what the old way of doing an installation is," says Nate. This is evident in the hardware throughout, which Nate hand-foraged at a local vintage hardware shop, and in the chalky veneer of the fireplaces, which are lined with old Belgian roof tiles cut on the bias. Patina is also an integral factor in the way they contrast the ornate and the gritty, the polished and the worn.

In contrast to the patina is the feeling only a fresh, light-filled shade of white can convey. They knew from day one they wanted a clean canvas on which to arrange their rich layers of furniture and objects. White also brought light and air into the home. We wanted the lightness of the space to match the soul of it," says Jeremiah. And, in turn, the home evolved. "She opened up every day in a different way. It was crazy." Nate and Jeremiah's home is a contrast of all these things— of freshness and patina, of light and mood. It is masterfully composed and artfully intimate. It celebrates that life is comprised of moments, and that embracing a serendipitous design journey is essential to creating an authentic home.

COME *Together*

An array of aesthetic periods and styles enlivens a room, but it can lose its vision without a focal point or anchor. When this happens, a controlled palette can bring cohesion and a unified purpose. In Nate and Jeremiah's living room, a traditional English bench can live with an Italian modernist sconce because the entire room is grounded in white, black, and earth tones.

"WE ALWAYS REACH FOR WHAT'S OLD, FOR WHAT'S TIMEWORN."

Stone Cold SHOULDER

Don't shy away from a porous, natural stone for fear of wear and tear. While Nate and Jeremiah's mantra may be to never polish anything, you might not be so comfortable with this laissez-faire attitude. A honed marble is a great remedy. The matte finish can mask rings and stains, making marks less glaring than on polished marble.

Elevate THE EVERYDAY

In the kitchen, forgo the stainless steel utensil holder in favor of a ceramic vessel you love. The practical and mundane moments of life should be beautiful and visually enriching, too. Every surface is an opportunity to express yourself and create vignettes that are personal and meaningful and, most of all, make you happy.

BRING THE *Outdoor* IN

A lichen-speckled outdoor concrete table set in a formal entry, rust-hued patio chairs in a wood-paneled library, and nineteenth-century French lanterns above a kitchen island lend Nate and Jeremiah's home an authentic layer of grit and patina against otherwise polished moments. Outdoor furniture that has withstood the wind and the rain provides unexpected contrast.

"I LIKE AT LEAST A MINIMUM OF TWO DIFFERENT MOMENTS IN ANY ROOM."

THINK *Locally*

Consider commissioning a local artist for something truly custom. Nate and Jeremiah found a decorative painter to turn the lush trees right outside their window into a mural in their master bathroom. Local art schools are a good (and budget-conscious) place to look for talent. The cost may be surprisingly competitive with wallpaper.

JENNA

FACT SHEET

Jenna Lyons:
Designer

Children:
Beckett

SoHo, New York, NY

Classic Loft
Built in 1909; renovated in 2014

Specs:
3,700 square feet
3 bedrooms
4 bathrooms
Kitchen/great room
Laundry room
Wardrobe room

RESOURCES

Beloved Antique Dealer
GALERIE HALF (*Los Angeles*)

Contemporary Designer or Shop
ANNA KARLIN (*New York*)
SAWKILLE CO. (*Rhinebeck, NY*)
ATELIER VIME (*Provence*)

Favorite Linens/Bedding
SFERRA
OLATZ
CUDDLEDOWN PILLOWS

Go-To for Tabletop
CASA DE PERRIN

Paint Brand/Color
FARROW & BALL
FINE PAINTS OF EUROPE

Online Destination for Decor
SUNNY'S POP
PLAIN GOODS
GRAANMARKT 13

Favorite Gallery, Flea Market,
or Auction House
1STDIBS (*online*)

"I love a sense of history in something. I love a patina, I love seeing someone else's touch, or seeing a stain, or seeing a nick or a chip. Materials get soft and they get round and they change color," says Jenna Lyons, a titan of style who transcends genres and trends (and who needs no introduction, really), of her lifelong appreciation for the timeworn that underpins her vibrant sense of design. I admire her sense of style and humor, her incredible business savvy and brazen risk-taking, and her passionate embrace of imperfection. It is no surprise that her homes past and present embody these incandescent personal traits and have proven fodder for countless aesthetes who swoon over her colorful, singularly personal point of view that breaks with convention.

A long stint of Brooklyn brownstone living informed Jenna's list of prerequisites in the search for a new home, namely that she wanted it to be all on one floor and large enough to accommodate the "main parts of life," like cooking, eating, hanging out. A proper SoHo floor-through loft fit her square footage requirement but little else. Unfazed, Jenna transformed it according to her penchants—French architecture, oversized crown moldings, and unfinished herringbone floors. She embodies the skill and confidence to repossess such a space.

When you walk into the apartment, there is so much to take in visually that your eye doesn't land on any one thing. This is not accidental, but rather a testament to Jenna's immense skill at layering. A Serge Mouille sconce peeks out

"I REALIZED THAT TAKING A CHANCE AND TRYING SOMETHING NEW WAS PROBABLY MORE VALUABLE THAN JUST STAYING WITHIN THE BORDERS AND WHAT EVERYBODY ELSE HAD DONE."

from behind a jungle-motif Dimore Studio screen; a leopard-print pouf sidles up to a pink Milo Baughman sofa. There is an artful mastery and playfulness in her placement and mélange of objects, materials, finishes, and patinas, yet this particular mix still reads bohemian. The way Jenna famously married sequins and camo mirrors her rule-breaking tendencies at home.

Jenna deliberately disrupts the symmetry of the architecture by hanging her artwork off-center, or even leaning it on the floor; it feels revelatory and unexpected, but more important, the eccentric placement highlights the work. After finding a Milo Baughman sofa, the anchor of the main living space, she altered its original design by removing the tufting and upholstering it in a pink cotton velvet. "In my job, I got used to having to say, 'This is what we're gonna do, it's gonna be okay, we're gonna try it,'" she says. "Taking a chance and trying something is probably more valuable than just staying within the borders and what the rules are." But her decisions are not half-baked. She spent hours poring over a cascading ombré of pink swatches to study which shade was best in various light temperatures throughout the day and evening, and in all sorts of weather patterns.

Green and pink—a combination that has a decidedly preppy reputation—is a recurring color pairing in the home. However, here it reads as anything but. It's made fresh and cool in Jenna's hands: An Aldo Tura pale malachite-hued goatskin cube cozies up to the pink sofa; avocado-green lacquer covers the powder-room walls; French eighteenth-century thread-bare peridot mohair chairs are sprinkled throughout the living room; even a menagerie of plants fuse the home in this surprising color palette. She credits Dimore Studio for influencing

her brazen color choices. "I'm so taken by their unapologetic color mixing and unusual textures and combinations."

At the nexus of fashion, art, design, and travel, Jenna naturally brings these elements into her home. She commissioned floating brass-clad bedside tables in homage to Donald Judd, and a bathroom at the Gritti Palace in Venice inspired her to source monumental and vigorously veined marble for her own. Jenna is a soothsayer, channeling and filtering ideas between the various disciplines. It is part of a magical aesthetic equation that separates her as an original. "When people are like, 'That's so cool!' I'm like, 'Great! It wasn't intentional,'" she says. Her admirers, meanwhile, wait with bated breath to see what she might do next—unintentional or otherwise.

With a profound love for the details and patina of French architecture, Jenna worked granularly with the contractor to finesse the millwork, moldings, extra-tall doors, and high doorknobs (she is five eleven, after all!) to reflect that appreciation. In all of the finishes Jenna chose throughout the home—the unlacquered brass backsplashes, the honed marble countertops, the unfinished oak floors—she wants life to be visible. "I literally had long conversations with my contractor about making sure the floors weren't too perfect," she says. "I wanted them to wear enough to show spills and reveal the markings of people's footsteps walking down the hall." It is symbolic of the honesty of life she craves. Because she's imperfect, and she has always clung to that individual imperfection. "I've never felt comfortable looking perfect or being perfect; my taste is weird, and I couldn't make a perfect room if I tried," Jenna says. She learned that was her gold: Know thyself, and let your home be a reflection of what works for you.

ART *Show*

Paintings do not need to be predictably centered over a fireplace mantel or symmetrically aligned on a wall. Jenna's off-center and idiosyncratic method of hanging artwork—clustered on the floor, breaking the moldings, lined along the windowsills—feels effortless and adds unexpected interest, drawing your eye in.

EXPRESS YOUR *(Stylish)* SELF

Start with a statement piece and then layer the accessories, supporting colors, and pattern. Jenna's pink Milo Baughman sectional is undoubtedly the focal point of the living room, but it doesn't dominate. Secondary colors and a duo of prints (the jungle-motif screen and the leopard pouf) make the whole room come together in a lively mix. A neutral paint color holds them in place.

Outside THE LINES

If you have twelve-foot ceilings, why settle for an eight-foot door? Door surrounds and decorative molding can extend past the actual door frame, offering verticality and a sense of grandeur. If you're considering new millwork, build the surround past the door break to trick the eye as Jenna has done here.

All BOOKED UP

Keep it simple when it comes to books, especially those used for reference, research, or frequent reading. Color coding might look cohesive but isn't great when you're searching for something. Jenna's bookshelves are first and foremost utilitarian, allowing a basic system to search and find. One shelf, tilted down at an angle, provides an opportunity to display and rotate her favorite pages. Plus, it makes an interesting foil to the late-nineteenth-century mahogany center table.

"I LOVE A SENSE OF HISTORY IN SOMETHING. I LOVE A PATINA, I LOVE SEEING SOMEONE ELSE'S TOUCH, OR SEEING A STAIN, A NICK, OR A CHIP."

LET THERE BE *Light*

While decor choices usually come after construction, lighting is the exception to the rule. I urge you to purchase your decorative light fixtures at the onset of your renovation, as Jenna did. The grand Venini chandelier dictated the central location for the electrical box over Jenna's kitchen island. The two side-by-side wall sconces on page 64 offer another example. Prevent the costly headache of rewiring and patching walls by sorting out lighting and electric placement first. Your bank account will thank you later.

Salty DISPOSITION

Unlacquered metals like bronze and brass are initially shiny and gold. The material will naturally age over time. You can accelerate the oxidation process by allowing the material to engage with the elements outdoors—or by spraying the metal with saltwater, as Jenna did to coax the green patina on the baroque-style bronze vanity legs in her master bathroom. It mimics ocean air, rapidly speeding along oxidation. Think Statue of Liberty!

Flatter BY IMITATION

While you may not be able to buy your favorite artist's blue-chip artwork, it doesn't mean you can't celebrate their spirit at home. Look to your most beloved artists for design inspiration. Donald Judd's minimalist, monolithic style proves fodder for Jenna, who commissioned her floating brass bedside tables as an homage to the artist.

SIGNE

FACT SHEET

Signe Bindslev Henriksen:
Architect and Designer

Soren:
Finance

Children:
Nicolas Roy, Vincent, and Feiina

Copenhagen, Denmark

Built in 1897, National Classicism
with a hint of Italian Renaissance

Specs:
3,000 square feet
4 bedrooms
1 living room
1 dining room
2 bathrooms

RESOURCES

Beloved Antique Dealer
OLIVER GUSTAV *(Copenhagen)*

Contemporary Designer or Shop
VINCENZO DE COTIIS *(Milan)*

Favorite Linens/Bedding
AIAYU: LIGHT AND
    CRISP COTTON—AND IT'S
    SUSTAINABLE!

Go-To for Tabletop
ROYAL COPENHAGEN
CERAMICS FROM JAPAN

Paint Brand/Color
ST. LEO *(Copenhagen)*

Online Destination for Decor
OLIVER GUSTAV STUDIO
THE APARTMENT
THE LINE

Favorite Gallery, Flea Market,
or Auction House
NILUFAR GALLERY *(Milan)*

Something about Copenhagen lights an incandescent fuse in me; the intersectionality of food, design, and lifestyle profoundly resonates, and I suppose it's not surprising that several of my dearest friends hail from this sophisticated Nordic city. Having these connections opened up the city's design beacons for me, and this included Signe Bindslev Henriksen, of the architecture firm Space Copenhagen, and her family apartment. Although we had never met, I had been in Signe's orbit for years and had cultivated a deep admiration for her style, which is best described as extreme elegance. Everything in the apartment is her art—every gesture, every composition, every detail. And like her home, Signe exudes ease, grace, and calm.

There is a nostalgic feeling in Signe's apartment, which is located in a nineteenth-century building. Streams of light pour in from a dramatic wall of arched windows, overlooking an abundantly verdant park, and cast shadows on perfectly positioned furnishings, many designed by Signe herself. She left no detail unconsidered in this rental apartment. Even in a space where an architect cannot make structural changes, she deployed an arsenal of facade and decorative improvements. A fresh coat of paint, black stain on the floors, new stone countertops, kitchen cabinets, and radiator covers reinvigorate the apartment. Most of all, her thoughtful design and art choices make this home most decidedly her own.

"I LIKE DIVERSITY. I LIKE THAT THINGS HAVE A SOFT SIDE, BUT ALSO A MASCULINE SIDE. I LIKE TO BLEND THESE CONTRASTS."

A controlled palette of black and white evokes simple, thoughtful restraint. Even with the dramatic tonal contrast, all is easy on the eyes. Each piece is so evidently imbued with intention both in its very being and in its placement: the curvaceous, sensual furniture pieces are as elevated and integral as the paintings on the wall. The home revolves around balance—softness, femininity, angularity, and masculinity. "If there's something very decorative," she says of her approach, "then I have something very sharp. It's a constant feeling of yin-yang in everything I do." Even the sculptural light fixtures teeter-totter on this tension. They are not primary lighting so much as they summon atmosphere. The living room's Apparatus cloud fixture, airy and ethereal, punctuates the bold, black lower half of the room. In contrast, the dining room's black Serge Mouille's muscular and leggy tentacles oppose the white, classically scrolled medallion that holds it.

There is intention in everything—and yet nothing feels contrived. You can imagine Signe asking herself two questions with every decision: Does this piece move me? Do I absolutely have to live with it? Even the salt in Signe's well-used kitchen is placed within a beautifully oxidized vessel. In the midst of our shoot, Signe disappeared. She returned with tea in a breathtaking Royal Copenhagen pot, toasty almonds having just departed the oven, and pears piled high in a gorgeous bowl with a dainty mother-of-pearl knife for slicing, all of which was delivered on an antique tray. It sounds fussy, but it wasn't; in Signe's casual attitude, it is apparent that this is simply how she lives. Signe poignantly says it's essential to only have pieces in your home that speak to you viscerally. "You should be able to say in a split second whether you like something or not." I love this sentiment in thinking about the dialogue in your home. While each piece must be conversational, it must also have a voice of its own and be able to speak for itself.

Signe describes her creative process as a way to define herself. She constantly investigates new furniture, technology, and ways of engaging in lifestyle spaces. This is how ideas and subsequently new furniture are born. When Signe cannot find what she is seeking, she creates it. "I don't see design as a project I draw, install, and finish. Rather, it's a playground where things can be under constant development." This home is a workshop, one in which she tests furniture in various states of production.

Signe has amassed furniture, objects, and art over many years, an exercise underpinned by consistent calibration. Her mantra is to design out of sincere love. With that approach, you can undeniably trust your instincts, even mingling the super modern next to the nostalgic. The only repetition here is the cohesive, calming thread of black and white. "I need my house also to be a place where I can close the door and not feel overly bombarded visually, because I also need to charge there," she says. "I need to be able to dwell, like a small temple, you know?"

*White*WASH

Blue chip or otherwise, if you treasure your art collection, as Signe does hers, allow it to shine. There's a reason why all galleries have white walls. White won't compete with your artwork. Paint your walls white to highlight your beloved pieces of art, allowing them to steal the show.

Northern LIGHTS

Chandeliers should not be a primary light source, but rather an atmospheric moment that helps establish the mood of a room. Decide what you want a space to be, and use chandeliers to either amplify its natural disposition or contradict it. Signe highlighted the loft-like airiness of her living room with an ethereal, soft, and romantic light fixture. She detracted from the monolithic quality of the dining room by deploying a sparse, leggy, and sculptural fixture to center the space.

FACELIFT

Signe's apartment is a rental, but you would never know it. While she couldn't adjust any structural elements, that didn't stop her from claiming the space as her own. Changing the face of things—from fresh paint choices, to wood stains, to radiator covers—can have a huge impact and eradicate the feeling of a transient, rental apartment.

CHANDIGARH, INDIA LE CORBUSIER
PIERRE JEANNERET

GALERIE PATRICK SEGUIN

RULE *of* THREE

Vignette styling got you stumped? Here, Signe canvases her coffee table with six stacks of books in a grid, four of which are then complemented by decorative objects. Consider rules of three: the composition of three objects offers aesthetically pleasing variation; this can also be seen on Signe's windowsill and is a

"I DON'T SEE A PROJECT AS FINISHED, BUT RATHER IN CONSTANT MOVEMENT."

Opposites ATTRACT

Beautiful interiors thrive on contrast, as we see in Signe's apartment. Consider this exchange of opposing values in your own home by contrasting masculine, rectilinear artwork with feminine, curvaceous furnishings, for example, or juxtapose ebony dark floors with crisp white walls. Place a gritty object next to a slick modern piece of design. Create friction in the home while highlighting the individuality and integrity of each piece in it.

Gritt-y PALACE

Pierce the perfect—break monotony by infusing an unexpected element of grit. If your space is pristine and modern, insert an imperfect, timeworn, or irregular object like the paint-chipped cabinet Signe has in her slick dining room. Rough-hewn wood or oxidized metal are great elements to contrast polish, ensuring a room won't be predictable or one-note.

DIVIDE *and* CONQUER

It is important that both you and your partner feel your home is a reflection of your tastes and interests. Distinguish territories within your home so your space reflects both sets of values and doesn't become a relationship battleground. Signe, the architect, selected the furniture and finishes, while Soren found and curated the artwork. She got the floors; he got the walls—a match made in heaven.

BLACK *Out*

———

Give consistency, structure, and drama to a space by staining or painting your floors one cohesive, dark color. Dispensing with rugs altogether, Signe stained the herringbone floors black throughout her apartment and chose larger pieces of furniture in a similarly dark color palette. This device grounds these elements to nearly recede into the floor, allowing more sculptural, lithe, and softer decorative pieces to come into focus.

ROBIN AND STEPHEN

FACT SHEET

Robin Standefer and Stephen Alesch:
Founders and Creators of Roman and
Williams and RW Guild

Shadmoor, one-hundred-acre wood
Montauk, NY

1955 Northeast sea cottage

Specs:
Main house:
1,200 square feet
3 bedrooms
2 bathrooms

Studio:
800 square feet
2 bedrooms plus a ceramics
and wood shop

RESOURCES

Beloved Antique Dealer
PAULA RUBENSTEIN *(New York)*
GALERIE HALF *(Los Angeles)*

Contemporary Designer or Shop
BLACKMAN CRUZ *(Los Angeles)*
THE NEW CRAFTSMEN *(London)*
GRAANMARKT 13 *(Belgium)*

Favorite Linens/Bedding
FRENCH ANTIQUE
SFERRA
RW GUILD

Go-To for Tabletop
RW GUILD
JAPAN AND DENMARK ARE
   ALSO FAVORITES

Paint Brand/Color
SCHROEDER PAINT
FINE PAINTS OF EUROPE

Online Destination for Decor
EBAY
RAGO

Favorite Gallery, Flea Market,
or Auction House
BONHAMS & BUTTERFIELD
   (Berwyn, PA)
RAGO *(Lambertville, NJ)*
MARCHÉ PAUL BERT
CLIGNANCOURT
   (Saint-Ouen, France)

I first met Robin Standefer and Stephen Alesch of Roman and Williams in Montauk eight years ago; we had just bought our home in neighboring Amagansett, and the area was still new for me. I'll never forget being invited to their seaside retreat to celebrate the Fourth of July that year. I walked through a narrow pathway lined with wax-covered surfboards under an archway of unkempt, lush greenery punctuated by a twinkle of overhead lights. I could hear the waves crashing on the cliffs just down the road, smell the salt hanging thickly in the air, while the scent of grilled meat filled my nose. This is summer in Montauk—decadent, bohemian, and intoxicating.

This luxuriant mood is elemental in its simplicity, rooted by a kind of modernism not found in the severe white angularity of the city, but rather in the soil, the briny ocean, and the dramatic cycle of the seasons that Stephen and Robin have harnessed in their 1950s Cape Cod home. Simultaneously raw and artfully collected, the house seems deliberately considered yet so disarmingly casual. They like it that way. It allows their minds reprieve to wander.

"That unfinished quality helps your brain evolve in terms of new ideas," says Robin. "It's that sense of a laboratory, that everything is sort of always unfinished. There's always a new experiment; there's always something new to investigate." The ceiling is perhaps the best example of this. Upon moving into the house, Stephen immediately punched through the ceiling's drywall to expose the original unfinished warm wood framing and beams hidden beneath. It was their first design decision, and it speaks to the spirit of all that followed.

Robin and Steven have cultivated a sense of wildness in Montauk, which has become a workshop for their design business. The untamed style of their home inspires their work, and that work then informs their design process at home in

"MONTAUK IS ABOUT UNFINISHED THINGS. THAT QUALITY ALLOWS YOUR BRAIN TO EVOLVE IN TERMS OF NEW IDEAS—LIKE A LABORATORY."

a beautiful cycle. Their tambour-clad living and dining room walls are a brilliant example of this symbiosis. They spied the material in André Balazs' office elevator while working on the Standard. They decided to use it personally and professionally: raw and unfinished in Montauk; glazed like lacquer in the Boom Boom Room. Meanwhile, a dark, enveloping shade of blue, which Robin likens to being inside the belly of a whale, covers their bedroom walls. They found it so peaceful, it eventually inspired the wall color at Guild.

Elsewhere, gestural collections of objects and artwork fill every surface. In the living room, a wall of densely clustered seascape paintings are hung gallery style; while it may look like a lifelong collection of the genre, it was a design decision that Stephen and Robin made early on and hunted for aggressively, with a strict budget of $150 per piece. The result is deeply evocative of place and mood. In contrast, collections of curios discovered in flea markets, antique stores, and even in nature create tableaux in cabinets and on tabletops. Each collection, in its sheer quantity, proves purposeful and soulful. "I really think everybody needs their own cabinet of curiosity," opines Robin. In lockstep, Stephen says, "We try to build this into a lot of houses. A shallow cabinet that you can just fill through time. You never finish. You have to let it grow." Time, permanence, and patina figure powerfully in Robin and Stephen's approach.

For years, the sole pieces in the reception room were the brass-edged table that hailed from a bygone-era French bank and a gargantuan hippo skull that sat on the far right edge of the table. Even today, these pieces remain like anchors, impervious to change. New objects, textiles, and furniture slowly accumulate around them, but fundamentally, the home's vision and purpose have stayed the same. "We can build on things, but we don't like to gut stuff and start over," Stephen says. "Magical things happen when there's stability, like seeing something bleach in a window; there's something so beautiful about that patina. You put something out and just see how it changes."

This also speaks to their garden, which could be mistaken for a rambling swath of English countryside. "A sense of imagination, I think, comes from a little bit of the unknown and a little bit of the undecided, and that's certainly gardening," says Robin. "Planting seeds, then relinquishing control. You could put all the time and love in the world into certain plants in that garden, and nature will take it away." The lush, slow-lived life they have coerced from this home and the land on which it sits reflects Robin and Stephen's values. "Find your own kind of sincerity," advocates Robin, "and love of what you're creating around you so that you're layering it and building on it and not changing it."

DO THE *Math*

Sometimes subtraction, not addition, is what a home calls for. Robin and Stephen peeled back the drywall that was concealing the humble and beautiful wood frame and beams that lay beneath. The undone look gave the house a relaxed, rustic feel immediately—just what the couple was after. Remember that adding and layering is not always what the doctor ordered in home renovation.

COLLECT, *Collect*

A collection makes a home feel personal, lived-in, and intriguing. There is beauty in excess. A collection doesn't have to be expensive and highbrow, but rather objects that speak to you in some way. Investigate what your eye craves; over time, the pieces will take on new meaning, and the whole will be greater than the sum of its parts.

Pick YOUR BATTLES

Stephen and Robin had to spend a big chunk of their budget on new windows and doors; they decided to save by repainting the circa 1970s kitchen cabinetry a slick black, brilliantly leaving the bevel white to look like trim. Stephen's playfully and practically painted numbers on the cupboards offer a road map so that guests can easily locate coffee and other essentials.

"I THINK AS A CREATIVE PERSON IT'S SO ESSENTIAL TO REMAIN A LITTLE LAWLESS AND UNTAMED. A LITTLE BIT OF A WILDNESS IN YOU. IT'S CRITICAL, AND I THINK MONTAUK'S ALLOWED US THAT."

Stay GROUNDED

Take cues from the land that surrounds you and elevate the ordinary by fostering a dialogue between objects. Well-used paintbrushes, a vintage wood hand model, and a hippo skull can take on new life and meaning when paired with shells, rocks, driftwood, and foliage that are right outside your door. Celebrate the beauty that surrounds you, and root yourself to the earth. Creating vignettes with contrasting objects adds sculptural interest and curiosity to the otherwise mundane.

A ROOM OF *One's Own*

Country or city, house or apartment, make sure to carve out a space that brings you joy. Robin and Stephen use their Montauk home as a laboratory to allow spontaneous thought. While you may not have a rambling country escape, carve out a sacred niche in your home that is devoted to your interests or hobbies, or is simply a place to decompress your mind.

POWER IN *Numbers*

Commit to a concept and explore it in plentitude. Sticking to a small budget, Robin and Stephen amassed a large grouping of seascape paintings, which they hung together. It has a powerful impact, creating mood and signifying place.

Darkness FALLS

For all the talk about white, neutral bedrooms, a dark, enveloping color like a deep blue, black, or graphite can cosset and soothe. Stephen and Robin swapped out a shade of white in both their Montauk and NYC homes for a dark blue, finding the rich darkness sleep-inducing.

GABRIEL
AND JEREMY

"... I think our language ... has evolved from very reductive geometry to things that start to feel a little softer, and more sinuous, and are more complex curves, and are not just about straight lines." Gabriel Hendifar and Jeremy Anderson are the creators of the seductive New York–based design studio Apparatus and are dear friends of mine. "Apparatus" is a word that speaks for itself in the design community— they never follow a trend, but rather build their own fantastical and unapologetic narrative, forecasting and even defining what's next in design, texture, culture, and even shapes. They offer a reminder that design can be a talisman to transport and transform.

When I first walked through the door, I was immersed in their fantasy world of tactile decadence—saturated in color, every square inch is flooded with texture, sultry curves, and perfectly odd and unexpected objects. With its abundance of circles and spheres that playfully please the eye, I immediately coined the space "the House of Shapes." Most of all, the home is lush and highly personal.

When Gabriel and Jeremy first saw the apartment, though, it was an industrial loft with beams and pipes looming overhead. The couple yearned for distinct spaces within the apartment but didn't want to structurally erase its identity as a loft. So, using two columns as guideposts, Gabriel and Jeremy devised a modular system of freestanding wood dividers that don't quite touch the ceiling to delineate areas and defined moments. It wasn't, however, until a chance sighting of a 1960s Danish pastoral scenic mural at an antiques store in Hudson, New York, that the contours of the wall formed.

As a departure from their last apartment, which was neutral, textural, and tonal, Gabriel and Jeremy wanted to embrace their version of color: sophisticated and rich, but also dialed back and aged. The mural hit all of those notes. They knew they needed it, and the solution to make it fit was the catalyst that informed the direction of the home. To accommodate

"LIVING IN A LOFT, WITH A VIEW OF THE EMPIRE STATE BUILDING, WITH LOTS OF SHINY BRASS AND LACQUER THINGS, AND COWS. AND THEN A PASTURE. WHY NOT?"

the mural, they decided to curve the divider, which created a dining nook and offered a soft transition into the living room. The figures of the mural provide a dynamic, unexpected exchange with the more modern forms set against it, like the spherical, oddly anthropomorphic pottery Jeremy makes and the sculptural, elemental marble table designed by Gabriel. Brass accents glisten in contrast to the earthy tones that mingle in the mural, like the yolk hay bales and milk chocolate cows. "It became the thing that either drove the contrast or the harmoniousness of colors in the space," says Gabriel.

The living room is dense in shapes, which contrast in materiality and revelatory color combinations. Soft circular forms and angular shapes meet, like the amorphous, foot-like coffee table designed specifically for the space, and the bright, multifaceted aqua artwork by Robert Moreland. Circle-pierced Prouvé-inspired panel shutters flank each window, which they added for visual cohesion. "It's the idea of having a consistent perspective," remarks Gabriel. "I'm attracted to systems for living."

Elsewhere, offbeat objects punctuate formality and rigor, like a pair of "bartenders": male and female wood liquor cabinets that stand like two Egyptian sculptures on copper plinths from a hunting lodge in Maine. A wooden carved ram that

Gabriel purchased as a twentysomething in LA sits atop an art deco armoire. These objects hold sway over the couple and enrich the home with elements of personal histories and predilections.

The bedroom serves as a repository for long-fantasized-over influences. Gabriel replicated a leather coverlet after seeing one designed by Ward Bennett for the Agnellis' bedroom in Rome. Inspired by a show they had seen at the Prada Foundation, the walls are swathed in a sultry, wine-hued velvet, which turns the space into a decadent jewel box. ZAK+FOX velvet was made into panels and fitted to the walls by Jeremy himself. "It was a total DIY project," he recalls. A deeply intimate object—a diminutive oil painting of Jeremy's ear—hangs above the bed and masterfully beckons you into the space with its wily use of scale.

This triumphantly unexpected, imaginative, and dynamic home is a hybrid of Gabriel and Jeremy's tastes. None of it makes any sense, and yet the cohesive thread is woven into a masterful tapestry like only the finest weaver can do—it is all SO damn genius. Gabriel may have said it best: "You have an idea of where you think you're going to go, and then you find something."

Color SCHEMING

Allow a statement art piece to either drive the contrast or the harmoniousness of colors in your home. Here, a pastoral mural inspired the deep brown color scheme throughout, but it also allowed for a polarizing juxtaposition when paired with more modern, bright elements within the space. Cohesion and contrast always create intrigue.

Lofty IDEAS

A wide-open space, like a loft, can be intimidating to dissect into rooms. Allow architecture, like immovable columns, to guide you. Don't be afraid to experiment with dividers: the mobile, faceted wood wall here offers so much to the space—a distinct entryway, a more intimate dining room, and a place to hang art. Plus, you can always reconfigure it!

Lean IN

Pattern on pattern, tone on tone—don't be afraid to lean into sameness. In this case, the tonality of an art deco burlwood armoire set on a wood divider and wood floor may not be an obvious choice, but embracing a look—whether it's pattern, tone, or texture—can have a powerful effect.

THE ALICE IN
Wonderland EFFECT

Don't underestimate the power a strong shape can have in your home, especially when repeated and complemented by forms that bring it into contrast. Circles dominate this apartment—and sculptural, geometric forms play against its soft harmony, giving your eye multitudes to explore.

"IT'S ABOUT THE MIX, AND IT'S BEING IDIOSYNCRATIC, AND HAVING ENOUGH TENSION TO KEEP YOU ON YOUR TOES."

MAKE IT *Cozy*

Use a textural material to add warmth and intimacy in your bedroom. Here, Gabriel and Jeremy's use of velvet on the walls, doors, and even curtains truly envelops you. Of course, not all of us can use swaths of expensive velvet, so a textured grass cloth, wallpaper, or simple cotton can offer a similar luxurious feel.

MINIMUM *Maximum*

Play with the contrast of excess and minimalism. In the dressing room and bedroom, there are a plethora of rich textures, finishes, materials, and hues that read both rich and luxurious. The restrained use of a few furniture pieces, however, and a diminutive painting of Jeremy's ear over the bed, juxtapose the lavish materiality. Contrasting extremes yields powerful statements.

OLIVER

FACT SHEET

Oliver Gustav:
Creative Consultant;
Antiques Collector and Dealer

Østerbro
Copenhagen, Denmark

Built as a private art gallery and known
as the "Museum Building," it dates to
the 1920s.

Specs:
The design studio and showroom
are approximately 7,000 square feet.

RESOURCES

Beloved Antique Dealer
MY FAVORITE STORES
    OFTEN GO BACK TO FAR
    DESTINATIONS.

Contemporary Designer or Shop
THE GERMAN GOLDSMITH
    PETER BAUHUIS

Favorite Linens/Bedding
OUR OWN LINEN AND
    HEMP COLLECTION

Paint Brand/Color
WE MIX OUR OWN PAINTS
    MADE WITH NATURAL
    PIGMENTS.

Favorite Gallery, Flea Market,
or Auction House
GAGOSIAN *(New York)*
AVLSKARL GALLERY
    (Copenhagen)

There are certain people who enter your world and simply shift the paradigm, so unique in their art, they coax something deeply emotional from within you. Isn't that what art is, actually? This is how I feel about the singularly identifiable Oliver Gustav. Oliver's fantastical antiquarian eye, gift for composition, and distinctive sophisticated color palette coalesce at his eponymous showroom and exhibition space in Copenhagen's Østerbro neighborhood. There is such sincere passion, honesty, and timelessness to this series of rooms, which were formerly an art museum.

I've obsessed over Oliver, who is described in a multitude of ways—designer, creative consultant, curator, collector, botanist, artist—for years. Whether at his showroom, in an image on Pinterest, or in a shelter magazine story, Oliver holds hypnotic sway over you in a vividly sensorial, richly monochromatic, and tactile trance. I never knew him personally, however, until I came to Copenhagen to shoot his space, but he welcomed me into his museum-like world with the warmest, most jovial open arms; we talked about design, passions, and trusting your intuitive eye as we peered through the camera lens, styling ancient objects from Pharaonic Egypt to contemporary furniture by Faye Toogood and Rick Owens.

Oliver grew up in a collector's family—his great-grandfather lived in Indochina for twenty-five years, where he amassed unusual historical objects. He also had an amazing sense of color; Oliver thinks that much of his eye was transmitted through DNA. "I believe what I do can be seen as a part of my heritage," he says. The key to his design approach is never self-censoring, but rather reacting solely from his heart. Oliver doesn't second-guess, and certainly doesn't bother measuring or drawing a layout of a room. His mandate is to buy what you

"I NEVER PUT UP RESTRICTIONS FOR MYSELF. I BUY WHAT I LOVE. I BUY ITEMS BECAUSE I FIND [THEM] FASCINATING AND BEAUTIFUL."

love, period. "I never buy an item because it is 'something' in someone's eye. I buy an item because I find it fascinating and beautiful."

Oliver's work is a master class on how to play with scale and composition. He engages verticality, maximalism, and texture in vignettes in unexpectedly genius ways. In one instance, a marble column on a console and a textile haphazardly hung as art are situated next to a seventeenth-century African object. In contrast, he deploys an artful minimalism in the next scene: A large sofa sits alone against a massive wall, with a crumpled piece of metal hanging off-center above it. He also plays with perspective, like by placing chairs on top of shelving in his personal office so that he can admire their silhouettes and proportions; it celebrates their beauty over their function, and the unexpected placement creates precisely the intrigue that we all find fascinating.

His vision is thoughtful, guided by confidence and restraint. Oliver envelops your senses with collections and compositions that unite rare antiquities and stark contemporary pieces from designers like Peter Bauhuis and Vincenzo De Cotiis, who he represents. This is his true gift: fusing beauty through the ages and allowing it to be seen as one seamless execution.

"Often people enter the showroom and believe that every item is from the same space, time, or designer," he says. "But there actually may be a thousand years between an aluminum-cast stool by the Dutch designer Jan Janssen and a prehistoric Egyptian vessel. I get attracted to the same universe, and therefore the pieces still fit together despite millennia separating them." He also unites these pieces, which span thousands of years, by deploying a muted, dusty backdrop. It is a serene through line in his interiors, unifying his vast and varied collections. The richness of gray allows the colors to come through and sets a dramatic mood. Oliver's love of botany, trees, and nature is another consistency through the space, and of course, the designer's personal line of hemp- and linen-upholstered sofas and armchairs act as an anchor.

No matter the origin of each piece, everything exudes the same atmospheric calm and beauty, leaving you wanting it, wanting more, and engulfed in spellbinding contemplation. Oliver leads you on a journey through art, travel, and discovery. He mingles the muted with the saturated, color and shadow, death and life. He finds beauty in melancholy and celebrates the perfect tension between it all.

Gray's ANATOMY

The putty gray Oliver painted the showroom reads monochromatic, warm, and sophisticated. The objects in the store, many grounded in subdued tones, would lose their value on white, but feel nuanced set against a gray backdrop. Painting a room a singular dusty hue on the walls, ceiling, molding, and millwork offers richness while allowing artwork and objects to shine.

CLEAR *It* UP

Practice restraint and don't let a blank wall trick you into unnecessarily filling it. Oliver hangs a singular sculptural piece off-center above a long white sofa, and a painting and sculpture at the very edge of another one. These unexpected decorative deployments foster intimate moments. Negative space allows your eye to breathe and concentrates your attention on the quiet, personal vignettes within a room.

THE *Wild* CARD

The rule is, there are no rules. Oliver's approach to hanging does away with formula and measuring. Anchor the piece you wish to highlight and build around it with opposing shapes, textures, and sizes hung in a scattered, unpredictable way. Pair the rectilinear with the amorphous; pair the slick with the rough. Forgo convention by breaking spatial planes.

Show OFF

Rather than costly built-ins, consider an antique cabinet for double duty—serving as a decorative tableau for displaying objects and for practical storage. The worn, charmingly imperfect cabinet Oliver has in the showroom serves as a beautiful vitrine for a collection of vessels. While built-ins are meant to disappear, an antique cabinet can be a showstopper in and of itself.

*Heart*BREAK

Embrace the broken—use it. A fractured object you love—a splintered cup, a shattered dish—doesn't lose its value in your heart. Transform a broken vessel into a sculptural moment on a tabletop or stack of books. By repurposing the jagged and the damaged into something decorative, you foster that silent, intimate language meant to bring joy to your eyes.

"I DON'T REALLY THINK BEFORE EXECUTING, AND I NEVER DRAW A COMPOSITION."

ONE MAN'S *Treasure*

Amass what moves you. Oliver is a collector, hand-selecting that which excites and intrigues his eye—
objects both humble and sophisticated that span time and place. Pieces you collect, regardless of time
period or style, drive narrative, emotion, and history in an interior. They stand on their own, and in unison,
they tell a personal story about themselves, and about you, imploring conversation and visual interest.

TIP *the* SCALE

Introduce drama by juxtaposing scales. Oliver allows objects and art to battle by contrasting the diminutive and the oversized while intersecting the vertical. Elevate the unexpected by placing objects that belong on the floor to eye level. Overlap objects in a vignette and allow them to amplify and play off one another.

GIANCARLO AND JANE

GIANCARLO AND JANE

FACT SHEET

Jane Keltner de Valle:
Style Director, *Architectural Digest*

Giancarlo Valle:
Architect and Interior Designer

Children:
Roman and Paloma

Brooklyn, NY

Built in 1928 as a cardboard factory;
converted to residential in 1998

Specs:
2,300 square feet
3 bedrooms
2.5 bathrooms

RESOURCES

Beloved Antique Dealer
GALERIE JACQUES LACOSTE
(*Paris*)

Contemporary Designer or Shop
NILUFAR GALLERY (*Milan*)

Favorite Linens/Bedding
OLATZ

Go-To for Tabletop
SCULLY & SCULLY

Paint Brand/Color
PLASTER

Online Destination for Decor
CABANA MAGAZINE

Favorite Gallery, Flea Market,
or Auction House
WRIGHT (*New York*)

"It's really important to let yourself go and try to find the unexpected. It's an innate quality in everything we do. There's this level of discovery, surprise, and intrigue that has to be there," says architect and designer Giancarlo Valle of his design process. It's evident in the tactile, graphic, and layered home he and wife Jane Keltner de Valle, style director of *Architectural Digest,* conjured up out of a former concrete block in Dumbo's iconic clock-tower building. I felt a sense of nostalgia as soon as I walked into the building to visit them; I bought my first apartment at that same address nineteen years ago, and, in a sense, my love of design began there. It made Jane and Giancarlo's brilliant transformation of the space that much more appreciated.

The doors open up to a large, bright room filled with striking jewel tones, eye-catching sculptural furniture, and playful patterns. Nothing inside is accidental, yet nothing is contrived. As an architect and furniture designer, Giancarlo knows that for design to be successful, it has to be a conversation among styles, objects, and architecture. Antique tapestries cover the walls and iconic vintage furniture is interwoven throughout: a low Milo Baughman burlwood coffee table anchors the living room, and a Pierre Jeanneret Chandigarh desk cements the library. "We would stumble onto these pieces as they came into our lives and discovered them," Giancarlo told me. "We used them to anchor and build whole rooms around them." The couple's den, for instance, lacked direction until

"IT'S ESSENTIAL TO NOT DESIGN EVERYTHING ALL AT ONCE; REMOVE YOURSELF. LET SOMETHING GUIDE YOU TO A PLACE—IT LEADS TO SOLUTIONS THAT YOU JUST COULDN'T HAVE FOUND OTHERWISE."

they stumbled upon a Gae Aulenti salmon-hued marble table in an antique store.

Naturally, Giancarlo used his new home as an opportunity to mine his own design curiosities, including a wave motif that is recurrent in their apartment. "The motif is in some ways universal," explains Giancarlo. "You would find it in ancient Rome and again in the Inca empire, and in the fifties and sixties in Royère's designs. I was obsessed with trying to develop it further." In their home, it takes on a playful and novel quality, surfacing in the living room's built-in window seat, on the plywood stools tucked under the kitchen counter, and even in their children's bedroom on the shelving millwork.

Most striking of all, however, is the sense of intimacy the erstwhile industrial space now communicates. "We kind of embraced the weirdness," says Giancarlo. "The starting point was to balance this raw and refined aesthetic in a way that felt balanced and had a level of authenticity—and to treat the concrete in an honest way." While they accomplished this by filling the space with collected furniture, the materials and finishes used perhaps had an even more potent effect in softening the industrial.

In the bedroom, Giancarlo covered the walls in a velvety oyster-hued plaster, which is complemented by a panel of billowy white linen that hangs over the bed by two humble wood poles. This simultaneously softens the room and conceals the harshness of the ceiling beams. The beams were, in fact,

a point of contention; a feng shui expert had advised the couple that they inhibit energy. This cautionary missive sowed a kernel of doubt that the couple felt they had to resolve. They replicated the solution in the children's room, with a canopy of soft coral-hued fabric draping from the ceiling over the daybed. These two elements, intended as a compromise, became one of the best decorative devices in the home—proof that problem-solving can yield rich results.

The once-bare concrete apartment has evolved into a layered, rich home filled with art, objects, and history that belies Giancarlo's crafty resourcefulness. His addition of panel moldings on the living room walls creates an elegant, sophisticated effect, while inexpensive plywood was deployed throughout, at times left raw, whitewashed, or with a luxe parchment finish. In lieu of traditional pulls or knobs, he carved triangular cutouts to act as hardware—a nod to functionalist Shaker-style furniture.

A harmonious tension between the raw and the soft, the industrial and cultivated, makes Giancarlo and Jane's home surprising and uniquely compelling. The couple strived to create a soulful and romantic home out of space that was decidedly not. Slowly, each beloved piece informed where the next one should go, while a practical ingenuity guided and supported their process—one that continues to evolve. Their most valuable lesson? "Rome wasn't built in a day. Don't rush it."

Shake THINGS UP

You don't have to slavishly follow the period or style in which your house was built—it is your home, after all! Giancarlo sourced molding from his local Home Depot and installed it in his industrial loft; decorative art deco-style detailing in a converted warehouse isn't an obvious choice, but it yields unexpected elegance and fosters a new design dialogue between eras.

Three's COMPANY

Experiment with unexpected color combinations. In this living room, a primary red is complemented by two secondary, yet equally saturated colors—vibrant teal and mustardy olive. Set against a neutral backdrop, they work well together in their strong frequency and independence. Try tacking up a range of fabric swatches using this formula—one primary color and two secondary colors—to find which trio is the most intriguing.

Change FACE

Millwork is always the most expensive ticket in any home. If you're looking for an affordable alternative that still delivers the same stylish results, choose an inexpensive material like plywood and vary its finish to give a similar rich and unique appearance. Here, plywood was bleached in the master closets, left raw in the office nook, painted in the children's bedrooms, and stained to resemble parchment paper in the living room's window seat.

FLOORED

Don't forget that the floor is a canvas, too. Jane and Giancarlo immediately knew they wanted to change the flooring of the apartment to add warmth and balance out the raw elements of the loft. They chose a chevron pattern with a wide plank to bring scale to the space's high ceiling and jumbo columns.

Lead WITH WHAT YOU LOVE

Oftentimes, a room that lacks direction only needs that one star piece to turn it all around. When this happens, tap into your heart and allow something you can't live without to inform the rest of the room, just like Giancarlo and Jane did with a marble Gae Aulenti coffee table. It became the catalyst for the den's terra-cotta walls lined with a blue-black railing detail—an homage to the late designer David Hicks.

TEXTILE *Trick*

Fabric is not just for upholstery and curtains. The industrial ceiling of Giancarlo and Jane's apartment made the bedrooms feel austere, but a strip of plywood and a few yards of gauzy linen was a crafty and romantic solution to a feng shui dilemma. A canopy of fabric draping over the daybed in the children's room similarly provides softness and warmth.

"I THINK DESIGN IS REALLY SUCCESSFUL WHEN IT'S A CONVERSATION BETWEEN STYLES AND OBJECTS."

Cut IT OUT

While adding beautiful hardware would be the obvious choice here, this stylish closet design proves it doesn't need to be your default. A simple triangular cutout can replace handles and pulls, creating a visually captivating alternative. Consider this for built-ins, like kitchen and bathroom cabinetry. It will also spare your hardware expense.

STEP *and* REPEAT

Create visual continuity by repeating a motif throughout the home. Giancarlo and Jane duplicated an undulating wave motif—a design element that spans from ancient Rome to Royère—and applied it to the bar stools in the kitchen, the millwork in the children's room, and the bench that extends from the living room to the office. This seemingly simple design touch brings a sense of cohesion to the apartment.

ATHENA AND VICTOR

FACT SHEET

Athena Calderone:
Interior Designer. Visual and Culinary Storyteller

Victor Calderone:
DJ and Music Producer

Children:
Jivan

Amagansett
Long Island, New York

1960s midcentury modern

Specs:
2,200 square feet
4 bedrooms
3 bathrooms

RESOURCES

Beloved Antique Dealer
OBSOLETE *(Los Angeles)*
OLIVER GUSTAV *(New York/ Copenhagen)*
RUBY BEETS *(Sag Harbor, NY)*

Contemporary Designer or Shop
FAYE TOOGOOD *(London)*
MONC XIII *(Sag Harbor, NY)*

Favorite Linens/Bedding
RESTORATION HARDWARE VINTAGE-WASHED BELGIAN LINEN SHEETS

Go-To for Tabletop
K.H. WÜRTZ
SPECK AND STONE PLATES
CLAM LAB PLATTERS
GOOP GLASSWARE

Paint Brand/Color
KALKLITIR: MINERAL LIMEWASH PAINT
FARROW & BALL: WEVET

Online Destination for Decor
MARCH SF
FRAMA
SPARTAN SHOP

Favorite Gallery, Flea Market, or Auction House
CHAIRISH *(online)*
BRIMFIELD *(Massachusetts)*
HOLLER & SQUALL *(New York)*

"THIS HOME WALKS A FINE LINE OF RUSTIC AND MODERN. IT REPETITIVELY TOYS WITH EXTREMES, BUT IT IS IN THAT REPETITION THAT YOU FIND THE COMMON THREAD."

My Amagansett home brought much of my life, as I know it today, into focus. It unified us as a family, demanding that we slow down, connect to nature, and plant our feet in the sand. It has served as a workshop for me, allowing me to explore my own layered aesthetic interests, and it has brought me close to the earth and her seasonal rhythms, inspiring and shaping the way I cook and entertain.

This grounding force, a seaside reprieve from our hectic lives, has been our steady home through four apartments in Brooklyn. It is the backdrop where my experimentation in the culinary, entertaining, and design worlds solidified, and where I began to realize there was a common thread among what I assumed were very disparate interests. Within these walls, I realized I perhaps have a story to tell; EyeSwoon was born here—and the rest is history.

When we bought this home, however, it was caving in on itself and so engulfed in trees that the blue sky overhead was obscured. The inside was dank and moldy. But my, oh my—the architecture, with its clerestory windows and abundance of glass doors, was a Hamptons midcentury modern diamond in the rough (mold and dead deer in the pool notwithstanding). Although it wasn't in perfect shape, I knew it was the perfect project.

We hired our neighbor, famed modernist architect Paul Masi of Bates Masi, to oversee the renovation. As he focused on the architectural improvements, I began to explore the style and decor. This house offered me an invitation to trust my instincts, like a mandate to follow my unfiltered internal vision. This meant forgoing convention; I had no interest in living in a midcentury time capsule. Instead of amplifying the house's

obvious modernity, I was compelled to soften its edges with nonlinear, natural materials that would age and weather over time—or add elements that already had that patina. I wanted a space where the exterior and interior were seamless, encouraging carefree sandy feet and a revolving door of family and friends huddled around the kitchen to communally cook a seasonal meal from the nearby farm.

At the same time, I wanted a holistic approach that would unite decor to architecture. So this was my balancing act: to impose an electric juxtaposition—a tension that I always crave—while making the home feel visually cohesive. I remember seeing the home of interior designer Darryl Carter. His method of injecting contrast—using binary color, proper antiques with objects that feel worn, left a real impression on me. While his style, decidedly rooted in colonial and classical vernacular, was not mine, his sensibility in establishing intrigue, tension, and harmony helped guide my own process.

I knew the spirit I wished to conjure; it was simply a question of how to summon it. I found it in an unlikely, humble source—rope. From both a material and motif standpoint, rope became a rapturous fixation. I compiled a binder of rope inspiration images for our architect, Paul (these were the days before Pinterest, after all!), which included spools of vintage rope, primitive rope, leather gymnast rings, and an exhaustive section of Scandinavian rope and woven cord chairs, including Jørgen Hovelskov's harp chair. I wanted to use the utilitarian and natural, tactile material of rope in nonlinear ways. It turned out, rope would be the catalyst to negotiate a sense of harmony between the modernity of the architecture and the antique, patina-rich items I wanted to fill it with.

JULIUS SHULMAN
MODERNISM
REDISCOVERED

BRANCH *Out*

A floral arrangement need not be fussy, precious, or purchased from a pricey florist. Consider the charms of your own backyard and surrounding landscape. I frequently cut down tree branches like sumac, which grow with abandon in our town, and cull exuberant weeds to put in vases. They bring the outside in, offer drama, and most important, add a sculptural element to a room. Even when they wither, their beauty remains.

We came up with a crazy idea that neither I nor our brilliant architect knew how to execute: a rope ceiling that would also engage with the architecture. Paul devised a solution to engineer it using the most basic hardware-store three-quarter-gauge manila rope; he wove it between the wood beams and engaged the Danish cording detailing in places with functional purpose, like to hold our Lindsey Adelman chandelier or the vanity mirror in our bathroom. This kernel of inspiration ended up informing and guiding the design and palette of the entire home. It united the austere black-beamed ceiling to the warm, tonal, and soft wood design scheme that lived beneath it. It harmonized the tension—rope summoned the spirit.

While the rope ceiling was all about systems and repetition, my furniture process was less studied and more passionately impulsive. I followed my guiding principle: buy what you love, even if you do not know where it will live. Trust that it will find a home within your home. And so I began collecting items that told an unknown story. At the same time, in 2009, the design trend was all about reclaimed wood, as well as industrial antiques and obscure oddities, which gelled with my vision. I reveled in the hunt at local flea markets, antique fairs, eBay, and Factory 20. A 1930s button factory cabinet gave me precisely the grit and curiosity I was craving. But the piece that really took things in a head-scratching direction (even for my husband, who always trusts my design sensibilities) was the purchase of a sixty-inch-diameter Georgian table. It became the confounding focal point of the room, but only after I made the potentially insane decision to lop off two-thirds of it. I loved its color, its curved half-moon tapered sides, and,

most of all, the brown wood peeking through the ebony stain, imbuing my home with the allure of unknown history. A warm wood motif continued in the pile of logs I stacked vertically in a nook, as though they were an installation piece instead of fire kindling.

Last year, after nearly a decade in the house, I felt I needed to brighten things up and add a bit more balance, juxtaposition, and refined elegance. It is true that too much of one thing is never a good idea—the rough-hewn look coupled with salvaged industrial items and rustic finds was no longer working. My tastes, and the times, had evolved. I didn't want to wipe the slate clean and strip the home of its original identity, so instead, I used some strategic tweaks that would make a large impact visually, but not on my budget.

I slowly incorporated a few brass decor pieces and swapped out fixtures that boasted filament light bulbs. The blackened brick of the living room fireplace and two reclaimed wood accent walls also felt heavy and dated. Over a few weekends, Victor and Jivan removed the wood cladding and applied fresh drywall, then I plastered the walls with mineral limewash paint, which brought texture and levity to the space. The new tonal scheme—achieved with minimal investment and a little elbow grease—offered a dramatically fresh impact.

This home continues to be a workshop for me to experiment in. I will add, edit, and tinker with it, exploring refined elegance or injecting more grit as I see fit, but constantly seeking to balance the weight of things. It is my visual autobiography, telling the story of my evolution as designer, creative, woman, wife, and mother.

Unite AND CONQUER

Integrate architecture and interior design by choosing a unifying color scheme. I used the rope ceiling, my favorite architectural device here, black beams, and window mullions and replicated their tones throughout the house with furniture and textiles. It created a sense of cohesion and synchronicity between architecture and decor.

Preferential TREATMENT

Pick what you want your eye to focus on, and let the secondary pieces recede. My amorphous, sculptural coffee table was such a statement piece, punctuating the linear qualities of the architecture and much of the furniture, so I eliminated visual competition by pairing it with a neutral rug, a white, angular sofa, and a muted shearling midcentury chair. Bigger isn't always better—your largest piece of furniture doesn't have to steal the show.

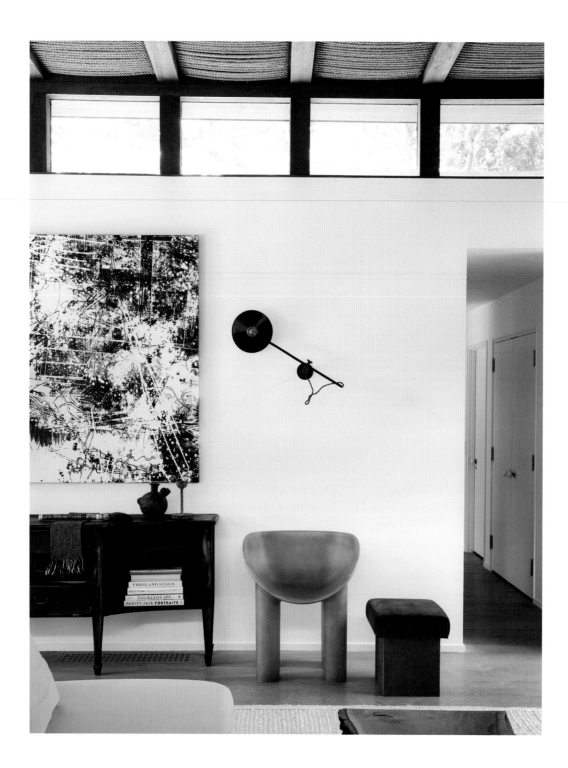

Don't SETTLE

I knew I wanted a rustic farm table as my dining table. I searched high and low for the ideal one—but they all came in too flimsy or too narrow for my family-style entertaining purposes. Instead of giving up, I took the dream to a local woodworker, who sourced the perfectly patina-rich reclaimed wood and created my ideal custom farm table, which had the concept I sought out and the functionality I needed. If you can dream it, someone can make it.

"I WAS IMMEDIATELY INSPIRED TO USE NATURAL, UTILITARIAN MATERIALS IN UNCONVENTIONAL WAYS."

Breathing ROOM

Make your kitchen another tableau for beloved and functional objects with open shelving. Follow the mantra "less is more" to avoid clutter, and give a breadth of space between items. Don't be afraid of uneven stacks, and play with verticality by grouping contrasting silhouettes next to each. Stick to a cohesive palette with opposing textures. Bring in a living element, like a potted plant, and limit your glassware to one or two styles, so it doesn't look haphazard.

Put IT TO BED

We all have financial limits when it comes to designing a home and deciding where to splurge and where to save. Each bedroom here has IKEA Malm beds (clocking in at less than two hundred dollars), which I painted monochromatic to the walls so that they simply and serenely disappear. It allows your eyes to focus on the decor of the room and the textiles on the bed. It is also an easy DIY trick—all you need to do is prime and paint; no sanding or stripping involved.

BROKEN *Symmetry*

Bedroom design often falls into formulaic, matchy-matchy monotony. Instead, play with symmetry and scale.
Here, in our master bedroom, I have matching sconces flanking the bed but disrupt their symmetry with two
radically different bedside tables—one a high industrial chest of drawers, the other a nesting duo of dainty,
low side tables in mixed materials. This combination of symmetry and lack thereof offers the room both
structure and unexpected interest, forcing your eye to wander across the space.

ONE *and* DONE

Choosing a systemic approach that engages material repetition is a brilliant way to unify a home visually—and save money. Blackened lava stone juxtaposed by the warmth of wood—a combination I spied while traveling in Greece—became the inspiration for my kitchen. When it came time to decide on the finishes for the master bath, which replicated the rope ceiling and clerestory windows in the main room, I realized applying the same materials in the kitchen would pull it all together. It was efficient, economical, and aesthetically cohesive.

WALLFLOWER

Don't always look to chandeliers, table, and floor lamps for your lighting needs. Sconces are an exciting and sculptural way to engage with lighting design, akin to illuminated art. In this home, I use them to establish symmetry and framework, centering them around furniture pieces or paintings I wish to highlight, and to introduce contrast through texture, materiality, or shape. A well-designed sconce has its own integrity, offering a singular beauty to a room.

PAMEA

FACT SHEET

Pamela Shamshiri:
Interior Designer

Children:
Reza and Basel

Studio City Hills
Los Angeles, CA

Built in 1948, Rudolph M. Schindler
historical midcentury modern—
titled Lechner House

Specs:
3,700 square feet
4 bedrooms
4 bathrooms

RESOURCES

Beloved Antique Dealer
JF CHEN

Contemporary Designer or Shop
CHARLES DE LISLE *(Sausalito)*
GIANCARLO VALLE *(New York)*

Favorite Linens/Bedding
CUSTOM *(for clients)*
SOCIETY LIMONTA *(for myself)*
LEONTINE LINENS *(New Orleans)*

Go-To for Tabletop
HEATH CERAMICS

Paint Brand/Color
FARROW & BALL

Online Destination for Decor
SHED *(Healdsburg, CA)*

Favorite Gallery, Flea Market,
or Auction House
LIEF *(Los Angeles)*
GALERIE HALF *(Los Angeles)*

"I'm a person of traditions. I love repeating things year after year. We really recover and hide out here on the weekends, and it's the gathering place for my family," says Pamela Shamshiri, perfectly encapsulating the feeling of stepping inside her Los Angeles home, a Rudolph M. Schindler midcentury modern marvel. Pamela, cofounder of Commune and founder of Studio Shamshiri, brilliantly walks a fine line in this indelibly personal home. Rife with attention to detail and ceremonial acts, it feels entirely contemporary and lived-in—a refuge for her and her boys—yet it pays deep and thoughtful homage to the great architect whose vision delivered it.

Life is everywhere in this pristine home—a perfect contradiction. It's in the open cans of spray paint, left around for teenagers to graffiti the pool with. It's in the living area's cowhide rugs, which are easily folded up to allow for indoor skateboarding (!), big family gatherings, or yoga classes. Guitars and music sheets commandeer a corner of the living room, while Pamela's collections amassed from travel, like talismans from ancient places, mingle with ceremonial sage and beautiful fruit-filled wooden vessels from Africa.

What I love most is sensing the devotion and patience that brought this storied house back to life; it took Pamela seven years, after all. While she had wanted a slice of Los Angeles history to restore, she wasn't sure if she was up for the scope of this project. Every window and every door needed replacing, and layers of paint and drywall obscured so much of its original beauty. But she decided to take on the challenge,

"I BEGAN EMBRACING THESE IDIOSYNCRATIC SOLUTIONS AND USING A MIX OF REALLY THOUGHTFUL DESIGN WITH PRETTY LOW MATERIALS."

and it became a springboard, informing her work at Commune as she dug deep into Schindler's archives. "There were so many lessons that I took with me," she reflects, most important of which was Schindler's devotion to humble materials compellingly deployed; she's embraced it ever since. "Things feel more approachable and relaxed when you use a mix of high and low. I think if it's all high, it's not as easy to live in," she says.

This was the philosophy that underpinned the renovation of the house, which also happens to be one of Schindler's last works. To get back to the essence of this conceptually brilliant, materially humble home, Pamela painstakingly stripped away layer upon layer of drywall and paint instead of adding, a process she refers to as "The Excavation." Incredibly, hidden beneath the drywall, she unearthed the architect's notes on the project—down to the most minute of details—written on the original plywood walls. She also removed the marble fireplace mantel, under which lay Schindler's dramatic steel fireplace, dormant and intact.

Though Schindler's fingerprints are all over the home, it is animated by Pamela and her family. She doesn't live in the shadow of its past. Infused with layers of rambunctious teenage boys, it has been brought up to contemporary ideals in the kitchen and bathroom, both of which she enlarged and splurged on. Paying historical homage and living today need

not be mutually exclusive, she maintains: "It's important for people to see that you can respectfully have a great kitchen and great bathroom and live in a historic home."

What truly defines this home is the surrounding nature, amplified by the angular, diagonal windows that draw your eyes out and into the canyon. It feels quite a bit like perching in a glorious treehouse. The geometry of the architecture, built-ins, and furnishings creates a dynamic where they nearly recede, allowing textiles and art to come into focus. More striking is the adherence to tonality that Pamela embraced. Taking cues from Schindler's celebrated plywood, nearly every surface in the house amplifies the hue of that warm, simple wood.

The architect's fascination with caves as the original dwelling proved irresistible fodder for Pamela, who loves camping and the majestic sequoia indigenous to California. She mined these touchstones, along with Anasazi cultures, to inform her approach and celebrate the spirit of this home. "It's such a California house. You sit there and see a treescape out every window. From any direction you look, it's a whole vista of trees." All of these ingredients formed the narrative of this historic and highly personal place. "It's a lot like cooking," says Pamela. "If you get the right ingredients and measure correctly." And that she does, fusing high design with low materials. Schindler surely would have approved.

Outside THE LINES

Your home should facilitate your lifestyle. Pamela's great room is an active place—she hosts yoga sessions, large family gatherings, and even skateboarding teenagers indoors. So she put all of her furniture on wheels and chose easily foldable cowhide rugs, making her house nimble enough to accommodate her family's diverse activities. By laying her cowhide rugs down on a bias, she is highlighting the unconventional shape of the room. Consider layering organically shaped rugs in unexpected orientations, particularly in a nonlinear room like Pamela's.

HIDDEN *Secrets*

If you live in a historic home and are considering a renovation, do your homework first—research old floor plans and photographs if possible, and strip away to see what might be hidden beneath the layers of paint, plaster, and drywall. Brilliance is often obscured by time and passing fads. You might be surprised at the pristine condition of hidden original elements, like Pamela was with the steel fireplace and plywood walls.

Sacred HEART

Devote a space to things you love, and encourage your children to do the same. This home is full of rituals that bring Pamela joy and the travels that have colored her aesthetic. Populate surfaces with meaningful objects that create a sense of intimacy and personality and, more important, provide happiness.

"WHILE WE'RE STEWARDS OF THE HISTORIC PLACE, WE HAD TO MAKE IT OUR OWN."

History LESSON

Resuscitating a historic home shouldn't banish you to another era in time. As Pamela says, "We bathe and cook differently today." Don't be daunted by a kitchen or bathroom that doesn't reflect your modern-day needs—there are ways to faithfully and thoughtfully change a home's footprint for comfort without making it look like a sore thumb. Use the materials and color palette of the home's original design as your guidepost, as Pamela did with tonal tile and cabinetry.

Lean IN

Accentuate and amplify tone to create drama. Pamela, taking cues from the humble plywood that so inspired Schindler, continued the pale wood tonality throughout the rest of the home, even mimicking the colors with choice of bathroom tiles, bathtub, flooring—right down to the accessories. Using a singular tone or material in repetition can provide a grand and holistic visual statement—and even an inexpensive one.

DOUG AITKEN 100 YRS

MAJA HOFFMANN   FRANÇOIS HALARD   RIRKRIT TIRAVANIJA

Cave IN

One of Schindler's most important principles is that an interior should offer a sense of calm security—like the cave did for our ancestors. While Pamela's home feels a bit like a bright treehouse, her bedroom is a departure, with walls and ceiling saturated in a dark hue, evocative of an enveloping, cozy den. Consider deep paint colors for your bedroom, like moody gray or inky navy, that ensconce you and offer protection.

FACT SHEET

Danielle Siggerud:
Architect and Founder of
Danielle Siggerud Architects

Pets:
Our dog and cat, Alf and Carla

Copenhagen, Denmark

Seventeenth-century
converted townhouse

Specs:
4,100 square feet
4 bedrooms
4 bathrooms

RESOURCES

Beloved Antique Dealer
DANSK MØBELKUNST
   (Copenhagen)
GALERIE H. BRÉHÉRET B.
   DESPREZ *(Paris)*
GALERIE HALF *(Los Angeles)*
OLIVER GUSTAV STUDIO
   (Copenhagen)

Contemporary Designer or Shop
MICHAEL ANASTASSIADES
   (London)
PIERRE YOVANOVITCH
   (New York)
NILUFAR GALLERY *(Milan)*
DIMORE STUDIO *(Milan)*
CARUSO ST. JOHN *(London)*
DAVID CHIPPERFIELD *(London)*

Favorite Linens/Bedding
SOCIETY LIMONTA

Go-To for Tabletop
K.H. WÜRTZ PLATES
SORI YANAGI CUTLERY
JOCHEN HOLZ GLASSES

Paint Brand/Color
ST. LEO *(Copenhagen)*

Online Destination for Decor
THE FUTURE PERFECT
1STDIBS
AZUCENA.IT

Favorite Gallery, Flea Market,
or Auction House
SUNDAY-S GALLERY
   (Copenhagen)
ADORNO GALLERY *(Copenhagen)*
BUKOWSKIS *(Auction House–
   Stockholm)*

"AS AN ARCHITECT, YOU HAVE A MAJOR RESPONSIBILITY— DESIGN-WISE AND MATERIAL- WISE, IT SHOULD STAND THE TEST OF TIME."

Stepping into the seventeenth-century townhouse of architect Danielle Siggerud is a study in minimalism, contrast, and warmth. The serene home she shares with her husband was originally the Royal Naval Base and sits directly on the canal, overlooking the beautiful harbor of Copenhagen. Danielle, whose Norwegian and Thai heritage offered her an understanding of cultural contrasts, studied within a stone's throw of her current home at the Royal Academy of Fine Arts. Engaging the old with the new, dispensing with trends, and following the mandates of function but executing form with élan coalesces her principles. Danielle's precision with details, however, is striking. The thoughtful attention that went into material choices, layout, and how she engages in her space was undoubtedly shaped during her time working under John Pawson.

In Danielle's home, old and new mingle with ease, both architecturally and decoratively. The building's original seventeenth-century beams, which had been obscured during previous incarnations, lend a statuesque, rustic framework to the home. They act as a skeleton, supporting the contemporary elements Danielle has orchestrated around it. "We wanted the beams to be like a statement, like sculpture," she says. The townhouse boasts a deep footprint but doesn't benefit from four exposures. In an effort to maximize sunlight's reach, Danielle chose materials that either amplified it or had a porous quality for light to filter through. Extremely thin-profile steel-framed glass doors and staircase rails keep the home open, while also providing a contemporary, urban contrast to the centuries-old beams.

Danielle's approach to design and architecture is complementary. She uses materiality to guide you through her home: designating the historical, the new, that which she wants to focus you on, and that which she wants to draw you away from. The original walls are delineated by a sandy, plaster terra-cotta-like three-hundred-year-old antique treatment, while the new walls are a minimal, disappearing white. "I always show what is actually original and what is old," says Danielle. "I'm not trying to make something look like each

Vincent Van Duysen: Complete Works

GEORG JENSEN A TRADITION OF

BEAM *Me* UP

If you are fortunate enough to have a historic home, celebrate it. Danielle amplified the three-hundred-year-old beams in this townhouse by leaving them untouched and choosing contrasting minimal white walls to "puff them up." Don't whitewash the beauty of patina.

other." Similarly, in the kitchen, she chose the most basic of Carrara marble to swathe her backsplash and countertops. It is not meant to steal the show, but recede, so you focus on the historical wall treatments and beams that loom above it. Her design narrative is quietly directional.

A devotion to minimalism underpins her style; however, Danielle also has a big family, and loves to cook and entertain. So she places a big emphasis on concealing the practical, adhering to the mantra "a place for everything, and everything in its place." In her bedroom, she installed doors that fold in on themselves, which conceal mundane necessities—like the TV, water kettle and faucet, and makeup table. "They are still present," she says, "it just makes your life a little bit easier." Danielle demonstrates a degree of self-awareness, confidently knowing how she lives and letting it lead how her space can most easily facilitate that.

Danielle has a poignant approach to the life cycle of furniture; she only buys vintage, and sells something if she chooses to buy a new piece so there's "circulation," as she

puts it. Her Buddhist Thai and pragmatic Nordic background are both synthesized and distilled in this responsible method. Danielle also embraces moments of romantic conceptualism. One of my favorite elements in her home is an asymmetrical elm root desk Danielle designed for her husband as a wedding gift. Two separate tabletops are supported by three trunk-like legs. "It is symbolic of their individuality, but they are unable to stand alone. Together, they become complete—referencing the love between two people," Danielle says.

I love this sentiment, as it corresponds to much of life, and it most certainly applies to design. It is this concept that I have tried to expound on in this book: examining single, unique facets—art, objects, furniture, textiles—that converge to create compelling personal spaces, singular to one person's journey. It is in the accumulation and orchestration of these single pieces that a picture is painted, forming a home that reflects its creator.

"IT WAS VERY IMPORTANT TO EMPHASIZE THE CONTRAST BETWEEN WHAT WAS OLD AND NEW."

Clean Up YOUR ACT

If you are a minimalist but also love to cook and entertain, pay thoughtful attention to the way you design the behind-the-scenes of your kitchen. Consider concealing everything—from the obvious, like knives and spices, to the bulky workhorse staples, like coffee makers and toasters. Danielle does this to a T, even having installed a secondary dishwasher to avoid unsightly plate piles.

Momento MORI

Flowers left to dry out become beautiful, organic objects that act as sculptural elements in your home. Danielle deploys their decaying allure on a number of surfaces throughout her townhouse to strange and elegant effect. Let your buds wither for a year-round sculptural arrangement.

Float BY

Don't necessarily put furniture pieces against a wall, particularly seating. Here, furniture floats at a remove from the wall, so you can move through the space more easily, and lends airiness to the townhouse. It also celebrates beautiful furniture by giving it a monumental quality, like Danielle's custom-made desk.

WALL to WALL

Highlight the original by juxtaposing the new. Establish a conversation between the historical and the modern by choosing two wall treatments to designate time periods. Danielle applied a warm, sandy finish to the original walls and used a stark, clean white for the newly built. You don't have to have a unified approach to every surface in your home.

Room SERVICE

Channel the best of a hotel experience when appointing guest rooms. With the guest rooms located on the fourth floor, Danielle thoughtfully put an electric tea kettle and installed a concealed kitchen. While a kitchenette might not be doable, consider the small details that make a person feel at home—coffee, slippers, or even a plush bathrobe.

Light WORKS

If you live in an apartment or townhouse that is very deep but lacking in four exposures, think about elements that will carry sunlight through the space. Pale wood floors refract sunlight in a way that darker wood would absorb it. A steel staircase and glass-paneled door—an urban, modern foil to the rustic beams—have thin profiles, allowing light to flow through the home.

FACT SHEET

Kearnon O'Molony:
Consumer Brand Investor

Kate Mack:
Casting Director

Amagansett, NY

Sculptural midcentury
modernism, built in 1967

Architectural Restoration:
Isaac-Rae Studio

Specs:
1,500 square feet
3 bedrooms
2 bathrooms

RESOURCES

Beloved Antique Dealer
PIÉR RABE *(Stellenbosch,
South Africa)*

Contemporary Designer or Shop
MABEO *(Botswana)*

Favorite Linens/Bedding
SERENA & LILY

Go-To for Tabletop
THE CLAY BUNGALOW

Paint Brand/Color
THE WHITEST WHITE

Online Destination for Decor
CHAIRISH
1ST DIBS

Favorite Gallery, Flea Market,
or Auction House
ROSE BOWL FLEA MARKET
(Pasadena)
CAPITOLIUM ART *(Brescia, Italy)*
LIVEAUCTIONEERS *(online)*

"For me, the holy grail is finding things that look good that you can live in. I never want anything that I am precious about," says Kearnon O'Molony of the decorative mantra that guides his spectacular Andrew Geller–designed, dune-nestled house in Amagansett. Despite being neighbors and having many shared friends, we had never met. The moment I stepped into his home, I understood what this modernist masterpiece was all about—part and parcel of why we had never crossed paths. You see, Kearnon and his fiancée, Kate Mack, never leave, and why would they? Rather, a carousel of friends arrives, and a typical day of surfing (the beach is just down the road), reading, napping, backgammon playing, and communal alfresco cooking ensues. "It's like rinse and repeat," says Kearnon, who hails from Cape Town in South Africa.

This narrative of nature and summer's splendor is the focal point of the way Kearnon lives here. A resplendent plentitude of the season's bounty—fruits and veggies in every hue—overflows on the petite kitchen island like a Dutch still life. Reggae music engulfs the room from a record player that sits in the corner near the windows, a shrine to the slow and simple way of life here.

When I walk in, the cedar walls and cantilevered spaceship-like glass windows refract the rich, glistening light from the dunes, splashing gold and straw and every other shade of

"THE CANTILEVERED WINDOWS ILLUMINATE THE HOUSE AT DUSK AND DAWN—IT'S LIKE A LIGHT BOX."

the sun's yellow throughout the home. Seemingly, it is the essence of what architect Andrew Geller was hoping to imbue the space with—a porous boundary between the walls of the home and the nature surrounding it. The warmth of the cedar envelops you.

Setting this scene is pivotal to understanding the design and flow of the home. Kearnon fell in love with the geometry of the space, the feeling of living in a light box, and the simplicity and practicality of the built-in living system. "It made some things really easy," he says of the built-ins, including the thirty-foot sofa that starts in the living room and extends to the outside deck in one contiguous line, further breaking down the barrier between indoors and out and offering fluidity from one gathering spot to the next. Given Kearnon's penchant for hosting, it is also highly practical. From backgammon to bed, "What's a couch you can't sleep on?"

The built-in sofa is the linchpin of the room, guiding the rest of the furniture decisions and layout. Four or five pieces make the house, turning Kearnon into a meticulous editor. A patchwork of vintage Malian indigo, which he purchased piece by piece, covers the sofa. "I've always loved African textiles—it's in my DNA," he says. A dining nook with a stunning biomorphic-shaped charred wood Shou Sugi Ban–style table punctuates the end of the sofa, becoming a banquette.

The cedar walls, such an integral element to the home, were a challenge. "When I bought the house, the wood was orange; I wanted something that had less red and orange, and more kind of grays and browns. A little on the lighter side, but rich

with a matte finish," he says. He and a local wood specialist embarked on what he called a tortured twelve-step journey that included various stages of sanding, bleaching, staining, and waxing. In the end, "it got to a great place," he says.

The guest bedrooms on the main floor are simultaneously diminutive and expansive, benefiting from large, cantilevered windows that create fluidity between the landscape and the room. "There was not one second where I thought I needed to make these bedrooms bigger. I think that's the charm," he says. Guests, he adds, will often forgo their designated bedroom altogether in favor of the sofa. Kearnon even transformed one of the bedrooms into a luxurious guest bathroom.

The moment you cross the threshold to go upstairs, you enter another dimension. A crisp white stairwell leads to the master bedroom. A stunning play of geometry greets you, juxtaposing stark white and warm wood; the contrast is exhilarating and nearly cinematic. The minimal amount of furniture is held in place by the white lower portion of the bedroom; it nearly recedes, save for a thoughtfully considered safari chair and an African textile on the bed—a nod to Kearnon's roots.

There is such allure in the casual monotony of how days turn to nights, and nights turn into days. How meals cooked in his outdoor kitchen, like his South African braai, are the only punctuations of a seemingly endless summer. "It's central to a kind of living," Kearnon says. "As a South African, I grew up cooking outdoors. It's not uncommon for me to have thirty people around for dinner." And that, really, tells the story of this compellingly uncomplicated, strikingly beautiful beach home.

Break BARRIERS

If you have a deck, consider ways to make it feel like an extension of the interior living space, and vice versa. Kearnon's sofa doesn't stop at the glass windows that separate the living room from the deck, playfully tricking your eye and breaking the barriers between inside and out. This is a wonderful way to bring a sense of nature into your home.

GO *Natural*

There is a tendency in modern interiors to mask wood walls with paint, but you don't need to whitewash wood to make it palatable. Experiment with techniques, like Kearnon did, to achieve the finish you like. Stripping and bleaching can have both subtle and dramatic effects, preserving the original wood while making it your own.

"I HAD TO BECOME VERY METICULOUS, BECAUSE YOU DON'T HAVE THAT MUCH SPACE TO WORK WITH, BUT THE SPACE YOU HAVE TO WORK WITH IS AMAZING."

SEW *Strong*

If you dream of upholstering a piece of furniture in a unique, one-of-a-kind antique textile but are afraid of it fraying, have the textile knit-backed. An upholsterer can strengthen a textile by bonding a secondary fabric, offering resiliency and allowing you to upholster fearlessly, as Kearnon did with his beloved indigo textiles from Mali.

DNA

Design is a unique blend of two worlds: the space and you. Infuse your home with your heritage and history. While so few pieces of furniture are in Kearnon's house due to the built-in nature of the space, the pieces he does have—ceramics, artwork, and textiles—are rich in meaning, reflecting his South African heritage and his affinity for surf culture. The convergence of these styles makes the home feel unique and extremely personal.

FADE *Away*

Painting hallways and stairwells a different color is an elegant way to signal transition within a home. Kearnon breaks from the warm wood of the house in the stairwell to his bedroom, which he had painted a crisp, Grecian-bright white. In addition to creating a beautiful contrast, it offers an uncluttered, seamless portal to the private part of the home, allowing the mind to reset.

KICKING IT *Old-School*

There is something incredibly charming about the analog nature of Kearnon's seaside retreat; the record player and a projector for "movie night" eliminate mindless channel surfing (that should be reserved for waves only!). If you're designing a vacation home, consider forgoing modern technology and letting the house be a real haven of decompression from the digital grind.

MONASTIC *Mood*

A simple bedroom—one in which only a comfortable bed, light, and bedside table
live—designates the room as a sacred sleep space. Kearnon goes ultra simple in the
appointment of his bedrooms, creating a calm, intimate, and inviting place to crash,
while fostering socialization in the communal parts of the rest of the home.

PAY *Homage*

While there are certainly times to break from a home's original identity, there are also instances in which you are best served to honor the architect's original intent. In Kearnon's case, Andrew Geller built the house to reflect and refract the light from the dunes. Any serious changes would have obscured the beauty of this device. Consider original intent before you take a battle-ax to an architectural home.

STÉPHANE AND PIERRE

FACT SHEET

Stéphane Garotin and
Pierre Emmanuel Martin:
Founders of Maison Hand,
Interior Designers and
Restaurant Owners

Ainay, a historical neighborhood
where most of the silk merchants
used to live
Lyon, France

French classic with bas-reliefs,
built in 1851

Specs:
1,500 square feet
3 bedrooms
3 bathrooms

RESOURCES

Beloved Antique Dealer
AXEL VERVOORDT *(Belgium)*

Contemporary Designer or Shop
BDDW *(New York)*

Favorite Linens/Bedding
SOCIETY LIMONTA

Go-To for Tabletop
ASTIER DE VILLATTE

Paint Brand/Color
ARGILE PEINTURE OR PURE
& PAINT FOR 100 PERCENT
ORGANIC COLORS

Online Destination for Decor
WE ARE NOT INTO ONLINE
PURCHASES. WE PREFER
TO TOUCH.

Favorite Gallery, Flea Market
or Auction House
LE SENTIMENT DES CHOSES
SCHOOL GALLERY *(London)*
GALERIE RX *(Paris)*

"DECORATING IS LIKE COOKING. YOU CAN HAVE THE BEST BOOK FROM THE GREATEST CHEFS, BUT IF YOU DON'T KNOW HOW TO COMBINE AND MIX THE INGREDIENTS, IT HAS NO TASTE."

I was first introduced to the immensely traveled, perfectly collected world of Pierre Emmanuel Martin and Stéphane Garotin of Maison Hand through Instagram. Partners in life and work, the French incarnate couple run a restaurant, design firm, and shop. It was a vignette photographed on a mantel in their home, however, that prompted me to brazenly ask them to open the doors of their circa 1851 apartment in Lyon's historic silk quarter. When I arrived, I was like a hunting dog, sniffing the trail of a pair of Brancusi-esque white sculptural objects that had so captivated my eye on Instagram. Of course, the sculptures were not for sale, but I am grateful they led me to Pierre and Stéphane for this book.

Not only do the couple's design penchants profoundly resonate with me, but they, too, share a deep love of food, cooking, and entertaining. I am always drawn to people who explore these two complementary passions, which have a symbiotic relationship in my heart. Their kitchen manifests these sister

interests—at once a practical, generously appointed space and a tableau for decorative objects that reflect their love of travel. It was also the first architectural change they made to the apartment. "The kitchen was located in a small room in the back. As we love to have friends over to cook, we immediately knew we wanted to dedicate a nice space to it," says Pierre. They relocated the kitchen to a street-facing room, but retained the wall separating it from the living room so as to preserve the original paneling and moldings. They installed a Boffi kitchen with open shelving to display their collection of crafts from around the world. "We always like to mix everything. It was a way to exhibit our collection and contrast the raw, cold materials and marble," says Stéphane.

Throughout their home, they distinctively treat raw materials with refinement. "We are more attracted by raw materials than precious ones. If we could, we would live in Brancusi's workshop," says Pierre. Textural linen curtains with a fine

THE *More* THE MERRIER

Decorative lighting sets mood and ambience. Floor lamps, table lamps, and sconces both illuminate and offer character and sculpture to a room—and are one instance in which one can never have too many. Be sure to vary scale and finish if you combine them on the same surface.

hemstitch pool to the floor, while roman shades made of gauzy linen boast unexpected polish. There is a sense of delicacy, precision, and thoughtful repetition to the way in which they elevate the simple. It is not a surprise they are drawn to Noguchi lanterns, of which they have several. Humble material is carefully and artfully manipulated to create something so simple, but so complexly sophisticated and elegant. They seem to thrive on this razor's-edge balance.

Craftsmanship and travel shape the contours of the home. Rather than grouping objects by country of origin, however, they devised vignettes driven by palette and form. Basalt-colored Japanese teapots mingle with a decorative black cross brought back from a trip to Mexico. Rattan baskets woven in Southeast Asia sit alongside indigenous Native American terracotta pots. Stéphane and Pierre are able to find the through

line that unites them, building a language based on aesthetic commonality and opposition.

This home also reflects the history of their relationship. The couple, who met in Morocco, fell in love with a textural Berber rug. Unable to take it home, they returned years later to find the vendor had saved it for them. Now in their bedroom, it grounds their most intimate space, a reminder of the shared history. As for the plaster pair of sculptures that led me here, their origins remain unknown. Pierre and Stéphane have attempted to track down the signature on the work to no avail. "Everyone wants to know more," says Stéphane, "but they're a mystery." And therein lies the beauty of the hunt, of finding the one piece that speaks a language meant for your eyes alone, calling you to it out of obscurity.

KEEPING *Grounded*

Plants offer so much to an interior. They bring in life, a sculptural moment, verticality, and even an element of the unruly. Overscale potted trees offer an intangible quality that amplifies the beauty and depth of a space. Plants deliver a verdant reprieve year-round, but especially lift your home—and spirit—in colder months.

Birds OF A FEATHER

Arrange collections and objects using color to keep them looking unified. In Pierre and Stéphane's kitchen, a grouping of diverse ceramic vessels and baskets collected from all over the world hew to shades of black, terra-cotta brown, and white. The effect, though, is not cluttered.

ALL WHITE *Everything*

White is a color, too, and is a fascinating tone through which to explore texture and variation. In Pierre and Stéphane's windowsill, an assemblage of ceramic and paper sculptural objects in shades of white feels rich and varied, focusing your eye on form, texture, and tonal nuance. Group together white objects in a variety of tones and textures; this monochromatic study will convince you that this color is anything but boring.

Déjà VU

A strategically placed floor-to-ceiling mirror can deceive the eye by enlarging the room, bringing in light, and multiplying objects you love. Here, a mirror leaning against a wall in the entry lightens up a dark hall and reflects a Noguchi standing lamp—giving the space a pleasant sense of déjà vu. Large-scale mirrors work wonders in amplifying light and form.

Extra LAYERS

Layers of texture lend bedrooms the cozy feeling they deserve. This room could seem monastic in its simplicity—so few items are in it—but instead feels richly warm. When it comes to bedroom design, layer on the textiles with a variety of diverse blankets, sheets, pillows, and rugs in textures ranging from open weave to dense, nubby, and fluffy.

VANESSA

FACT SHEET

Vanessa Alexander:
Principal and Founder,
Alexander Design

Point Dume
Malibu, California

1950s Spanish Colonial
designed for clients

Specs:
5,500 square feet (all buildings)
3 bedrooms in main house,
plus gym, office, media room,
kitchen, and living/dining

RESOURCES

Beloved Antique Dealer
GALERIE HALF *(Los Angeles)*
BLACKMAN CRUZ *(Los Angeles)*
JF CHEN *(Los Angeles)*
OBSOLETE *(Los Angeles)*

Contemporary Designer or Shop
APPARATUS *(New York)*
VINCENZO DE COTIIS *(Milan)*
OLIVER GUSTAV *(Copenhagen)*

Favorite Linens/Bedding
SOCIETY LIMONTA
ALONPI *(for cashmere)*

Go-To for Tabletop
RW GUILD

Paint Brand/Color
FARROW & BALL:
    AMMONITE AND RAILINGS

Favorite Gallery, Flea Market,
or Auction House
CARPENTERS WORKSHOP
    GALLERY *(London)*
WRIGHT *(Chicago)*
R & COMPANY *(New York)*

This magnificent, quintessential Malibu beach house almost ended up on the cutting room floor, along with the seventy-five palm trees that were felled in order to extricate it from junglelike obscurity. The owners, attracted to the oceanfront land but convinced that the structure on it was a teardown, found an unexpected, brilliant editor in Vanessa Alexander. The Los Angeles–based interior designer saw the potential in the 1950s-era Spanish Colonial and masterfully whittled away its neglected veneer to conjure up a laid-back, contemporary beach escape in line with her clients' lifestyle.

This home is one of two in the book where the designer is not the homeowner. This offers a useful lens for approaching design from a more pragmatic, less emotional approach. The clients had initially approached Vanessa's firm to clean up the various buildings as a temporary treatment while they devised plans to tear it all down in order to build a new, bigger, and better home. Vanessa began to assiduously clean it up, opening the floor plan while highlighting some of the remarkable original Spanish details. As this phase progressed, her clients were delighted to see the magic that lay beneath the years of neglect and had an about-face—they gave Vanessa the mandate to turn this down-on-its-luck property into the showpiece of a home it is today.

Clever use of materials guided much of Vanessa's process, like repurposing construction-scaffolding wood to connect all the various buildings. The pared-down, silvery patina of used decking softens the grandeur of the property to unite it with nature and the vast Pacific Ocean. "I always start by referencing the exterior of a building and the landscaping because I think that sets that tone," she says. This ethos revolves around humble and tonal textures that celebrate the nuance of the rocks, sand, and surf that lay just outside, which Vanessa then applies indoors.

"YOU MUST UNDERSTAND THE LAND ITSELF, THE WAY THE LIGHT HITS THE PLACE, THE BREEZE. EVERYTHING THAT GIVES YOU A SENSE OF PLACE."

For this home, the flooring was the first interiors change she embarked on. Indestructible, humble, and utilitarian concrete, applied throughout, visually unifies the home in a sophisticated way. Vanessa then took down the walls that divided the living room, dining room, and kitchen and opened up the main living space to breathe and bask in the California sunshine. In order to designate three separate spaces within the one large room, the designer used the same dramatic, tactile light fixtures to signal and center each area. Their oversized scale and textural rope, reminiscent of a straw sun hat, offer order to the large room. "They were beautiful but not overbearing," she says. "I wanted it to repeat without feeling boring." An oversized table with built-in banquette also helps form the contours of the space as it comes to life. She wanted one that "you can really live at, work at, play at."

In a nod to the salty ocean air that slowly weathers all it touches, Vanessa coated the marble countertops in acid, offering a matte texture patina that implores you to run your fingers over it. Plaster walls again provide subtle, imperfect texture, and are a "defining moment" of the home, and an inexpensive plywood bed frame lends a sense of interior architecture and practicality to the master bedroom while rooting it in earthy, neutral tones. In the kitchen, lustrous, glazed zellige tiles line the walls and cover the hood, resembling the opalescent interior of a shell.

A neutral palette, Vanessa maintains, draws you outward and creates a porous barrier to the sea and surf—just what a Malibu beach house should be about. In a high-privilege setting, this color theory focuses you on what is important: the shocking blues and greens of the sky, the ocean, and Earth's bounty.

CONCRETE *Jungle*

Assess the functionality of your home first and foremost. These surfer homeowners wanted a place they could wander into with sandy, soaked feet. Water-soaked wood warps over time, so Vanessa encouraged the use of concrete flooring—a cost-effective, indestructible alternative that supports her clients' lifestyle.

BREAK IT *Up*

Symmetry is an important element to hold your eye, but once you establish it, break it. The peaked roof in this home establishes foundational symmetry, which Vanessa accentuates with pairs of flanking focal points, like kindling on either side of the fireplace and mirrors on either side of a picture window. She then contrasts it with furniture, art, and objects that have different silhouettes and scales, allowing your eye to dance around the room.

LIGHT *the* WAY

In one open space with several living areas, different light fixtures can confuse and distract the eye. Don't underestimate the power of repetition for lighting solutions. The same pendant, used three times, unifies the space and simultaneously designates distinct areas within one room. Vanessa hung each pendant high so as not to obscure the ocean views.

"THE FLOW OF A HOUSE CAN INCREASE ITS LIVING POTENTIAL."

MAKE IT *Sparkle*

Texture is not just for textiles. Glazed zellige tiles in the kitchen offer light, texture, and sheen to the space. While you may not want a color or pattern to overtly overpower the walls of your kitchen, a glazed tile modulates light and surface irregularities, offering discreet interest and character. Vanessa even had the hood clad in it, creating a cohesive, luminescent atmosphere.

Wood WORKER

A simple, large piece of wood can work wonders. Vanessa used a tall piece of pine plywood and ran it along the back wall of the master bedroom as a headboard. This inexpensive architectural device serves a decorative, unifying purpose, creates a shelf on which to lean artwork and objects, and offers built-in bedside tables.

KEEP IT *Simple*

Adhere to the practical and amplify the purpose of a room. In a TV room, consider a super-deep built-in sofa with a menagerie of cushions to line the wall, inviting you to dive in. Choose a workhorse coffee table made from humble materials that will beg you to put your feet up. A pair of tables also allows a room to breathe, rather than one large monolithic block.

Weather SERVICE

Use salvaged wood for outdoor decking. Vanessa sourced old scaffolding wood to build the clients' decks; the weathered wood had already lived a life. Wet and dried out, the decking left no room for ambiguity of how a new wood might change over time. Plus, the worn patina feels right at home, as though it's always been part of this beautiful house.

JEAN
CHARLES

FACT SHEET

Jean Charles Tomas:
Interior Designer

Saint-Sulpice
Paris, France

Built circa 1850 in "Second
Empire" style and designed
for a client

Specs:
2,000 square feet
2 bedrooms
2 bathrooms

RESOURCES

Beloved Antique Dealer
GALERIE ALEXANDRE
GUILLEMAIN *(Paris)*

Contemporary Designer or Shop
MARTA SALA *(Milan)*
JEAN ROGER *(Paris)*

Favorite Linens/Bedding
MERCI
ROUGH LINEN

Go-To for Tabletop
ASTIER DE VILLATTE

Paint Brand/Color
RESSOURCE PEINTURES.
  I USUALLY USE WHITES OR
  VERY LIGHTLY NUANCED.

Online Destination for Decor
I NEED TO SEE THINGS
  IN REAL LIFE. ;)

Favorite Gallery, Flea Market,
or Auction House
LES PUCES DE SAINT-OUEN
  (Saint-Ouen, France)
PIASA *(Paris)*

There is nothing quite like a classic Parisian mid-nineteenth-century apartment to conjure design goals. Replete with original parquet floors, ornate moldings, and tremendously high ceilings, this space easily sends you down a path of romantic yearning. Jean Charles Tomas, who had just struck out on his own in 2016, had this perfectly preserved apartment with which to launch his eponymous design firm. Moreover, his clients gave him carte blanche in shaping their home.

This apartment, situated on a quaint street, is an exercise in patience, yes, but also in irreverence. There is an electric tension here between the Haussmannian architecture that characterizes traditional notions of Parisian style and the contemporary, pared-down interior design. Jean Charles is an absolutist in both regards—in equal measure a faithful restorer and an ardent modernist. It is in these two elements that he created something compelling here. Had he followed the cues of the architecture, the home might have been predictable. Conversely, had he followed the taste of the furnishings and ended up in a modern, white box apartment, it would have read monotone. There is jolt in juxtaposition.

Jean Charles chose this apartment for his clients as he was seduced by the rare eastern and western exposures that illuminate the space and its period details. It also benefited from a grand, elegant perspective between the dining room and living room, but a set of double doors—original, classical, grand—separated the two rooms. It was the first decorative impasse he had to reconcile. Ultimately, he was able to justify their removal as they took up a tremendous amount of space

"I FIND IT VERY RIGID TO DESIGN AND DECIDE EVERYTHING AT THE SAME TIME. IF YOU DO NOT LET THE SPACE BREATHE, YOUR DESIGN WILL BE STAGNANT."

and, more important, obstructed the view. In their place, he designed bespoke brass-and-glass doors that provide privacy between the two rooms but also allow the light in. The doors, with their rectangular brass grids, are a decidedly modernist foil to the grandeur of the moldings.

Another architectural change Jean Charles pursued was turning a bedroom into the kitchen. With its marble countertops, backsplash, and floating shelf, the kitchen could have felt austere, but the designer softened the space by installing lush floor-to-ceiling drapery and an upholstered breakfast nook. The homeowners admit that this little banquette is the heart of the home. The Angelo Lelli ceiling fixture is a dramatic, unexpected statement in a kitchen—more domestic and decorated than functional and utilitarian.

After deciding which original details to retain and which to alter, Jean Charles hired only the best to execute the changes. To restore the parquet floor, he brought in artisans who renovated the parquet in Versailles. They dismantled every single piece, then numbered, sanded, and oiled them, settling on a more contemporary-looking patina, and installed them back in their original place—a labor of love well worth it. Similarly, to repair the water-damaged ceilings, he found traditional plaster artisans, who molded details to then re-create in their workshop.

There is an innate sense of balance—dark and bright, matte and shiny, sharp and sculptural, old and new—to Jean Charles's work. "I tend to be subtle on what's static—walls, ceilings, flooring—as it allows me more flexibility to play with textures and patinas." For this apartment, he decided on a color palette, picked the textural fabrics for sofas, banquettes, and pillows and the materials for the kitchen and bath, and worked with his carpenters to get the right patina on the American walnut wood finishes. No matter the changes he oversees, he likes to pay homage to its original state. "I like to keep an original piece in every project," he says. Here, a hand-carved original wood door was retained, which he had sanded down to leave raw.

Jean Charles credits his work as being an accumulation of academic study and life experiences. The mind-set of Henri Matisse, who believed that adults ought to nurture a childlike mentality, has also struck a chord with him. "The creativity we have as kids is fascinating; everything is possible, the only limitation is our imaginations." It is true that we lose this boundless nature as we grow up, and we must temper our adult brain so we don't lose our sense of possibility. "I hope that my style will constantly evolve and grow and change so that it is as much a reflection of myself as an individual as it is about what interests me."

Light WORK

Here, Jean Charles uses a chandelier almost like an axis, dividing the living space and dining space, signaling transition. If you are perplexed by the idea of too many light fixtures competing for attention in an open floor plan, consider one dramatic chandelier to designate areas and offer visual separation.

BEST OF *Both* WORLDS

In this gorgeously preserved apartment, it would be a shame to obscure the original herringbone floors. Jean Charles selected a rug that fits just under the front legs of the pair of sofas, ensuring a soft-underfoot living room, while leaving the rest of the floor bare. When choosing a rug, it doesn't need to cover an entire room, but should always unite a seating area.

"YOU HAVE TO TAKE YOUR TIME, WAIT FOR THE RIGHT MOMENT, UNCOVER THE RIGHT ANGLES, AND THEN WAIT FOR THE MAGIC TO HAPPEN."

Glass HOUSES

Glass doors can be a wonderful way of allowing light to flow, while maintaining division and a sense of privacy within a space. Initially, it was hard for Jean Charles to dispense with the apartment's original wood double doors, but he didn't want to forsake the light they obscured. If you desire both division and openness, glass doors enable that duality.

CIVIL *Service*

Civilize your kitchen. A built-in banquette in lieu of bar stools, soft linen drapery, fine art on the shelves, and chandelier lends the kitchen warmth and elegance, and makes the space feel like an extension of this beautiful apartment, as opposed to a service-only area. Bring in decorative elements—even textiles and upholstery—to soften your kitchen.

TIME *and* AGAIN

Allow color and materiality to repeat throughout the home for a cohesive narrative. Jean Charles used a deep marine blue, warm copper tones, and American walnut in upholstery, metal, and furniture choices. The varied application doesn't feel redundant, but rather subtly unified and purposeful.

PRETTY *Practical*

Wraparound vanity mirrors are an excellent way to refract light—and offer an additional POV when you're doing the important things, like putting on makeup or checking the back of your hair. The mirrors here multiply and amplify the light from the single sconce, as well as offer another perspective during the morning and evening routine.

LAURE

FACT SHEET

Laure Hériard Dubreuil:
Founder & CEO of The Webster

Aaron Young:
Artist

Children:
Marcel

East Village
New York, NY

Nineteenth-century townhouse

Specs:
4,400 square feet
4 bedrooms
3 bathrooms
1 half bathroom

RESOURCES

Beloved Antique Dealer
MARCHÉ PAUL BERT
SERPETTE FLEA MARKET *(Paris)*

Contemporary Designer or Shop
STEPHANE PARMENTIER, WHO
  IS DESIGNING AND CURATING
  THE WEBSTER HOME

Favorite Linens/Bedding
D. PORTHAULT
MY GRANDMOTHER'S HAND
  EMBROIDERED FOR HER
  WEDDING

Go-To for Tabletop
MURIEL GRATEAU PLATES
LOBMEYR GLASSES

Paint Brand/Color
FARROW & BALL: STONE BLUE

Online Destination for Decor
1STDIBS
EBAY

Favorite Gallery, Flea Market,
or Auction House
OSMOS GALLERY *(New York)*

Laure Hériard Dubreuil is the very vision of French style. Her effortless knack for melanging pattern, color, and styles has defined not only her personal ethos, but also that of her wildly chic multicity boutique, The Webster, and, of course, her East Village home. Her townhouse, which she shares with her husband, artist Aaron Young, and son, Marcel, is a deft interplay between preserving nineteenth-century ornamental New York and contemporary art and design. Above all, perhaps, it sings electric color.

Laure has always been attracted to places that have a storied soul. Having grown up in Bordeaux, she was drawn to the house's ornate grapevines carved into the marble fireplace mantels, the detailed crown moldings, and the original floor-to-ceiling antique glass windows with their subtle, wavy irregularities. Designed by James Renwick Jr., the architect behind St. Patrick's Cathedral, the townhouse itself harkens to another era. She took a preservationist's view in maintaining many of the architectural elements, but instead of dressing the part, Laure and Aaron use the home as a canvas on which to celebrate and explore their love of contemporary art and twentieth-century design. In fact, the couple initially bonded over art when they first met: Laure's most treasured contemporary painting in her former home happened to be the work of Aaron's close friend Ryan McGinley.

Laure is unapologetic in her risk-taking and trusts her eye implicitly—always inspired by the spaces themselves rather than the period specifically. After walking through the home's

Sense & SENSIBILITY

Pair the practical with the sophisticated. In Laure's family room, an oversized leather sofa is the perfect practical piece for her family to lounge on. Next to it, however, is a sculptural and collectible chaise longue. Your living spaces don't have to be one-note. You can include an impractical showpiece—as long as you are fusing the room in sensibility, beauty, and balance.

original set of iron gated doors, you are greeted by a vibrant red and white canvas by Aaron. It sets the immersive color block tone for the rest of the home, where each room seems codified by color rather than purpose. Red returns in the family room, where a pair of Jeanneret chairs are upholstered in a maraschino cherry–hued velvet, grounded by a strident red rug. In the formal living room, shades of blue, from the sinuous metal swivel chairs by Milo Baughman to the shaggy carpet, reign. The parlor floor living space is a duo of teal and pink, with tiger stripes thrown in for good measure. Her effusive zeal with color simply makes you happy.

Laure and Aaron are similarly irreverent when it comes to mixing metals, which is another signature throughout the home. The first piece of furniture the couple purchased together was Paul Evans's Skyscraper cabinet, a Mondrian-esque meld of gold and silver–hued blocks. This embrace of warm and cold metals recurs throughout the home, sometimes eliciting an art deco mood evocative of both New York and Miami, two formative cities in which Laure has lived and established her business. Collectible pieces, like Brazilian sculptural furniture and Italian 1950s lighting, as well as black glass coffee tables with a Scarface-like vibe, and of course their dense collection of artwork both by Aaron himself and by mentors and dear friends, form the distinctive building blocks of this home. Bold, architectural, and sophisticated, Laure and Aaron's townhouse is testament to creating a nonconformist space that is most decidedly personal and authentic.

The red room is where the family spends most of their time, and it perfectly encapsulates the antipodal nature of Laure's brilliance with the mix. While an indestructible leather sofa grounds one wall of the space, a highly collectible Oscar Niemeyer chaise longue, with its sinuous shape, doubles as an on-ramp for Marcel's toy car collection. It is his favorite spot to play in the house. While their home may look cultivated, nothing is precious. Everything here is a highly personal expression of Laure and Aaron's irreverent visual landscape, brought to life in vivid color and form.

"IT'S THE MIX THAT WORKS FOR ME. I COLLECT WHAT I LOVE AND TRUST IT WILL FIND ITS PLACE, IT IS WHAT I'M DRAWN TO AT THAT TIME. I'M NOT CONSCIOUSLY TRYING TO BALANCE IT, IT ALMOST ALWAYS BALANCES BY ITSELF."

Greatest ASSETS

Instead of pushing furniture up against a wall, anchor it to the center of the room. Position beautifully designed pieces of furniture to their best advantage; sometimes the back or side profile of a chair is the best part of it. Floating your furniture like an island also allows for visual breath and intimacy at the same time.

American HISTORY

Celebrate the architectural integrity of an old home. Laure decided to maintain the authentically wavy original window panes of her nineteenth-century New York home, despite its less-than-efficient barrier to cold and heat. She also decided to forgo window treatments to highlight the splendid crown moldings throughout.

No RULES APPLY

Let your walls become a canvas for all, representing different mediums, styles, colors, and sizes. Collect and display artwork with wild abandon, anything and everything that speaks to you, no matter if it "works" with other genres or styles in your home. The more the merrier.

LINE *Dance*

Curvaceous furniture adds unexpected sensuality and softness to a space. If you decide to go round, make sure to break the circle by adding a square, or another ectilinear piece, as Laure has done with a giant square coffee table that both moors and amplifies the opposing curvilinear pieces.

HOT *and* COLD

While it was once considered taboo, don't be afraid to mix metals in the same space.
Just as there is beauty and tension in pairing an object with patina and one with polish,
so too is there an electricity in marrying the sunny warmth of bronze and brass with
cool silver and chrome.

"THERE IS A FRENCH EXPRESSION 'KEEP THE HOUSE IN ITS SHOES,' IT IS A HOUSE WITH BEAUTIFUL BONES. THERE IS A RESPONSIBILITY WITH HAVING A LANDMARK HOUSE AND BEING RESPECTFUL OF THE HISTORY. IT WAS IMPORTANT TO US NOT TO DISRUPT THAT."

ACKNOWL-
EDGMENTS

"FOR A HOUSE TO BE SUCCESSFUL, THE OBJECTS IN IT MUST COMMU-NICATE WITH ONE ANOTHER, RESPOND TO AND BALANCE ONE ANOTHER." —ANDRÉE PUTMAN

Well, isn't that the truth—and the only way to design a beautiful home! But it also holds true if you consider yourself and those you surround yourself with to be your "house."

Throughout this book, the creatives I surrounded myself with were my house, my walls, my very foundation. Collaboration, always essential to my process, was instrumental in bringing *Live Beautiful* to life. It made what might seem like a solitary, lonely pursuit less scary, and certainly less daunting. It also provided a much-needed sounding board for me to distill the many ideas reverberating through my mind into a singular, nuanced, and layered point of view. Somehow, I was able to congregate a seriously talented group of people from various disciplines and perspectives to accompany me on this journey. They supported me, challenged me, elevated me, and prodded me to think critically throughout the process. I am forever grateful, thankful, and indebted.

SARAH MASSEY. Thank you for your careful, thoughtful editing of this book and your brilliance with helping me piece together the complex puzzle of layouts.

NICOLE FRANZEN. I love you and treasure our journey together. I can't imagine roaming the globe and capturing these glorious homes with anyone other than you. The way you recorded the visual experience of these homes is steeped in passion and grace—your impeccable eye brought these stories to life. We made a BEAUTIFUL book together and had a blast along the way!

MIEKE TEN HAVE. We sure did have fun wordsmithing (and eating) together, didn't we! What a privilege it was to write beside you—you were absolutely invaluable to the language of this book. Thank you for elevating and finessing my every word, even if you did have to teach me some new vocabulary along the way. Ha!

NICOLE TOURTELOT. Throughout the many frenzied moments I had while putting this book together, you remained steadfast and calm, like an anchor. I am eternally grateful for your wisdom and encouragement.

JORDANA MOSTEL. Oh boy, where do I even begin? We've been through so much together, we are practically morphing into one being, sharing the same idiosyncrasies and attention to detail. I could not have pulled this off without you. Thank you for being with me through every moment of this process. I love you madly, Jordy, and I cannot wait to see what else we conjure and create together.

NR2154 TEAM. I knew from the moment we met that you would design this book. I am in awe of your talent, craftsmanship, and ability to see even the smallest, hyper-granular detail. Thank you for bringing *Live Beautiful* to life, and for all the patience and beauty you poured into it!

THE ABRAMS TEAM. Thank you for your belief in me and for offering unbounded creative freedom. I am grateful for this opportunity you have given me.

COLIN KING. How did I survive before July 2018, when we met? You are the ultimate sounding board. After endless hours—whether on my living room floor or on a bed in upstate New York—laying out images and conceiving tips, you bring both brilliant insight and hilarity to this process. And, as usual, styling my house together felt a bit like creating with my Siamese twin. Oh, wait, does that mean we are triplets now?

JENNA SARACO. Our visual mind meld is nothing short of amazing. Thank you for always lending your eye and your extreme talent in finessing the visual details in my homes.

THE FEATURED CREATIVES. Thank you for opening your homes to me. I am a curious creature: I love nothing more than to understand how compelling design unfolds, layer upon layer, yielding a personal, rich home. I am filled with gratitude for our time together in your most intimate setting and for your generosity in illuminating the path you took to reach it.

AMY ASTLEY. Your support, generosity, and friendship mean the world to me—who knew spring break in Costa Rica would lead to such a rich personal and professional relationship! Thank you for writing the first words that lead readers into these pages.

EYESWOON READERS. I'd be nothing without you, your support, your guidance. We are in this together, always!

MARISSA CAPUTO + AIRE. I could not be more grateful to navigate this creative path together with you. Thank you for always seeing me.

KAREN ROBINOVITZ. You saw it first. You made it happen. Thank you.

JOHN RAWLINS. My mentor. My friend. My partner. Always pushing me, always guiding me. Thank you!

ELIZABETH ROBERTS. I pinch myself daily that I get to call this house my home. Thank you for embarking on this renovation with me. I am so fortunate.

PAUL MASI. Amagansett simply would not be steeped in the beauty it is without your ingenuity and vision. Thank you, Paul!

SACHA STREBE. Your generosity, wisdom, and insight were beyond appreciated.

GABRIELLE SAVOIE. Thank you for embarking on this process with me and for laying the groundwork for what would become *Live Beautiful.*

NATALIE GOAL + HANNAH SAFTER. Having your eyes and edits on my words gave me the confidence I needed, thank you!

MOM AND DAD. Your creative lens informed my own—for that and for your unconditional love, I owe you everything!

VICTOR CALDERONE + JIVAN CALDERONE. Our beautiful life and the homes we created together, just we three, are really where it all began. You two hold me up. Life is whole with you by my side. All I do, I do for you. You two bore the brunt of my frantic moments throughout this book adventure—and you love me nevertheless. True love. The truest, the fullest, the purest!

EDITOR
Sarah Massey

DESIGN BY NR2154
Jacob Wildschiødtz, Elina Asanti, Stefanie Brückler,
Nicole Irizarry, Katharina Andersen

PRODUCTION MANAGER
Rebecca Westall

TEXT WRITTEN IN COLLABORATION WITH
Mieke ten Have

Library of Congress Control Number: 2019936967

ISBN: 978-1-4197-4280-4
eISBN: 978-1-68335-875-6

Abrams books are available at special discounts when
purchased in quantity for premiums and promotions as
well as fundraising or educational use. Special editions
an also be created to specification. For details, contact
specialsales@abramsbooks.com or the address below.

Abrams® is a registered trademark of Harry N. Abrams, Inc.

ABRAMS The Art of Books
195 Broadway, New York, NY 10007
abramsbooks.com